Following seven years in parish m
was a Director of Ordinands in
2001 to 2007, before deciding to focus more fully on writing.
As well as two sets of reflections for Church House Publishing's
Reflections for Daily Prayer in 2008 and 2009, she has written
four sets of Gospel comments for the Royal School of Church
Music's *Sunday by Sunday* magazine, five sets of all-age worship
resources for Scripture Union's *Light for the Lectionary*, and a
set of seasonal prayers for *Roots* online resources. She lives in
Cumbria with her husband (a vicar) and four children.

*With thanks to the clergy and Readers of
Solway Deanery Chapter, who invited me to lead
their Advent Quiet Day in December 2010,
from which this book took shape*

WINDOWS ON A HIDDEN WORLD

Exploring the Advent landscape

Jane Maycock

First published in Great Britain in 2012

Society for Promoting Christian Knowledge
36 Causton Street
London SW1P 4ST
www.spckpublishing.co.uk

British Library Cataloguing-in-Publication Data
A catalogue record for this book is available from the British Library

ISBN 978–0–281–06509–7
eBook ISBN 978–0–281–06510–3

Typeset by Graphicraft Ltd, Hong Kong
Manufacture managed by Jellyfish
First printed in Great Britain by CPI
Subsequently digitally printed in Great Britain

Produced on paper from sustainable forests

Contents

———◆———

Preface

———◆·◆·◆———

December is always a bit of a challenge. There is something spine-tingling about the beginning of Advent, something akin to watching stars appear on a dark, cold night. These pinpoints of light reassure us that even though we can't always see signs of it, the rest of the universe is still there, and the earth still has its place in the celestial order of things. Yet something exciting is about to happen. It is something to do with God, and we are on the threshold. It is like being a child going to bed the night before your birthday. You know that soon there will be something great and exciting, but the time is not quite there yet – and that is where the struggle starts.

Far too soon Christmas begins to take over, and I find myself on a rollercoaster ride which sometimes seems to border on madness. The 'ups' include: the children's excitement; buying presents for them and anticipating their pleasure when opening them; making Christmas cake, Christmas pudding and mince pies; getting the Christmas tree in and decorating it; singing Christmas carols. The 'downs' also include the children's excitement and managing their expectations. ('But Mummy, I said Father Christmas would bring the laptop/Xbox/PlayStation!' Implication: 'Silly Mummy, that means it won't cost anything!') The 'downs' continue with Christmas shopping, and the cumulative effect of all the extra Christmas things in the last week of term, which make me feel as if I'm spinning plates but haven't time to remember why. This continues right up to and beyond Christmas Day, and takes in the complaints from those who come to church once a year for whom the Christmas carols 'weren't Christmassy enough'.

So at the same time as my surroundings become increasingly filled with twinkling light, I become increasingly aware of the darkness around me. At times it can become more than just a hint – there is a real fear of gaping darkness very close by. The rather too cosy images of warmth and light sharpen up my awareness of those suffering illness, homelessness, loneliness and death. I find I have moments of being acutely aware of fear and anxiety. These can find an easy focus in my love for my family – will they all come safely home that day, or will some terrible accident befall them? The inherent fragility of human life presses down. In this state there lurks the fear of discovering that somehow Christmas will prove to be hollow, that there will be nothing at its core. The happy contented feeling I often have as I make Christmas cake and puddings gives way to an awareness that in a few weeks it will all be over – gone, in the past. We will be into January, with its long weary waiting for signs of spring.

In the midst of all this, the capacity to be taken by surprise is thankfully as real as the gaping darkness at my shoulder. I remember with gratitude a recent occasion when two days before Christmas I was stopped in my tracks – whether up or down the rollercoaster I can't remember – by the Advent calendar. This particular one has a small book for each day, telling the story of the journey to Bethlehem over the course of the month. By 23 December the angels were addressing the shepherds, and it was my turn to read. In the utterly mundane setting of teatime for six at the kitchen table, I was suddenly struck by the fact that it was the glory of the Lord that shone around – not just 'a rather bright angel light', but the *glory of God*.

This is the glory that dazzled Peter, James and John when Jesus was suddenly transfigured before them, when he took them up the mountain and appeared with Moses and Elijah (Matthew 17.1–8; Mark 9.2–8; Luke 9.28–36). It is the glory from which human beings have had to be shielded in order to protect them, as Moses' companions discovered at Sinai (Exodus 34.29–35). This glory is the very brightness of the presence of God! If that is not exciting, then I don't know what is. One of the problems with the whole Christmas thing as I experience it, is that there is something huge going on, and we scurry round like ants, apparently unable to see the scale and beauty of the garden they inhabit. My lurking fear that perhaps it will all turn out to be hollow is perhaps to do with the fact that much of it *is* hollow, because we simply do not allow enough time or give a big enough space for exposing ourselves to the presence of God.

Long before Christmas itself, though, I am reaching out for the companions I need to keep me sane for the rest of the season. These friends help me hold on to what is at the heart of Advent and Christmas:

> Wellcome all wonders in one sight!
> Eternitie shut in a span,
> Summer in winter, day in night,
> Heaven in earth, and God in man.

These words were written by Richard Crashaw (1613–49), an Englishman whose life took him on a journey from Britain to Italy, where he died as a Roman Catholic priest while still in his late thirties. His words in this poem, and those of other poets referred to in this book, help me to stay focused on what is at the heart of Christmas – God's over-arching love for the world and all human life within it. Grasping the depth of this love takes us way beyond a simple focus on the baby Jesus in the manger. It helps us to examine our own response to God, to what he has done in Christ, and the way in which we shape our lives to follow him.

One hope for this book, then, is that it might have that effect of pausing the rollercoaster and stopping us in our tracks, if only for a short time each day. It is intended that there be a general sense of progression. We begin Advent in a desert landscape, then move through three broad themes. The first of these might be summed up as 'clearing away the rubbish'. Both in the secular sphere and within the Christian tradition we often pick up ideas which we absorb without really thinking about them, and which do not necessarily stand up in the light of close examination. This is an opportunity to look at some of those things.

Within Christianity the 'four last things' have been traditional themes for Advent. These are Heaven, Hell, Death and Judgement. Considering these things is part of having a living faith: as we look back to what God has done in the past, so too we look forward to what we expect him to do in the future. This raises big questions of human life. Focusing not on the beginning but on the end means facing our own death, and highlights the question of what will happen when we die. Even here, however, we can find that we have assumed certain things which in fact are not true to Christianity, and this might be a time to look at them again. Yet there has to be a note of caution. These are big themes, each one worthy of a book in its own right. This is by no means an attempt to say all that could be said; far from it. Rather, we gaze on this Advent landscape through a window opened by others, and through which we can reflect on our own understanding.

The second broad theme is God's choice, which includes recognizing that both conflict and confrontation are core parts of Christian faith, and so of course of Christmas. The final theme encourages us to look ahead to the second coming of Christ. The word 'advent' does of course mean 'coming'. As we prepare to celebrate the first coming of Christ at Christmas, it is natural to think too about his second coming – this is an essential part of the Advent hope.

The choice of the biblical texts, and of the poems explored later on in this book, is of course personal – and is only a narrow selection of many possibilities. The exploration of the imagery used by the poets emphasizes the strength of the biblical imagery. Often, to try to take the imagery literally is to miss the point. Opening it up allows us to explore hard questions and emphasizes the fact that people have always used picture language to express things of which they are convinced, yet which are beyond our sight and only partially within the grasp of our understanding.

The three poems by Robert Southwell deserve to be more widely known, as do the words by Timothy Dudley-Smith. The adaptation of 'Hills of the north' has been, with these others, a great discovery of recent years. One of the things about all these words is that their authors are able to express much better than I can what Advent is all about. That is why they become something of a refuge every December, and why Richard Crashaw can have the last word here. These three verses come from his longer poem, 'A Hymne of the Nativity, sung as by the Shepheards'. They seem to me to sum up what I hope to convey in this book.

> We saw Thee in Thy balmy nest,
> Young dawn of our eternall day;
> We saw Thine eyes break from the East,
> And chase the trembling shades away:
> We saw Thee, and we blest the sight,
> We saw Thee, by Thine own sweet light.
>
> Wellcome all wonders in one sight!
> Eternitie shut in a span,
> Summer in winter, day in night,

Heaven in earth, and God in man.
Great little one, whose all-embracing birth,
Lifts earth to heav'n, stoops heav'n to earth.

To Thee, meeke majestie, soft King
Of simple graces and sweet loves,
Each of us his Lamb will bring,
Each his paire of silver doves!
Till burnt at last, in fire of Thy faire eyes,
Ourselves become our owne best sacrifice.

1 December: Isaiah 35

The wilderness and the dry land shall be glad,
the desert shall rejoice and blossom;
like the crocus it shall blossom abundantly,
and rejoice with joy and singing.
The glory of Lebanon shall be given to it,
the majesty of Carmel and Sharon.
They shall see the glory of the LORD,
the majesty of our God.

Strengthen the weak hands,
and make firm the feeble knees.
Say to those who are of a fearful heart,
'Be strong, do not fear!
Here is your God.
He will come with vengeance,
with terrible recompense.
He will come and save you.'

Then the eyes of the blind shall be opened,
and the ears of the deaf unstopped;
then the lame shall leap like a deer,
and the tongue of the speechless sing for joy.
For waters shall break forth in the wilderness,
and streams in the desert;
the burning sand shall become a pool,
and the thirsty ground springs of water;
the haunt of jackals shall become a swamp,
the grass shall become reeds and rushes.

(Isaiah 35.1–7)

What a place to start! This wonderful piece of poetry brings together images of contradiction, and stretches our understanding. It hints that there is something happening – something to do with the active presence of God. It places side by side ideas of anger and of salvation. It forges ahead with images of the renewal of diminished humanity and of the barren landscape. Its climax is the fulfilment of the promise hinted at earlier: through the coming of God there will be a highway through that renewed landscape, bringing joyful people into the presence of God. These themes of wilderness, of the anger of God, of renewal and of joy will come up more than once in this journey through Advent.

The wilderness seems like a good place to start too. After all, at some point in Advent we usually hear the voice of John the Baptist, out in the wilderness. Mark chooses to start his Gospel with John. All four of the Gospel writers pick up on the way in which John was spoken of by prophetic voices centuries before. People flocked to see and hear him, and the place they went to was the desert.

We may think of a wilderness as a bit of a 'no man's land', a place where nothing happens. Yet throughout the pages of the Bible we hear of this place as the focus for the presence of God – where God is experienced, and heard, and where God acts. It was in the desert places of Sinai that God forged the relationship with his people, and there that he taught them about holy living through the law he revealed to Moses. Only then were they ready to move on. By the time these words from Isaiah 35 were written, probably in the seventh or sixth century BC, many of the Israelites were all too familiar with the wilderness experience of exile. Far from home and with no autonomy, many were subject to foreign overlords and constraints on their religious practice. Leaping ahead again, it is of course to the wilderness that Jesus goes before embarking on his public ministry.

I have been to a real desert, but only as a tourist in Egypt with friends. We booked a place on an air-conditioned bus to take us from Aswan even further south to Abu Simbel, not that far from the border with Sudan. It turned out that 'air conditioning' meant simply that there was no glass in the windows of the bus. So for mile after mile the desert wind that sent tumbleweed rolling over the sandy, stony landscape, blew around us too. It was a wonderful experience. We were always on the move, however; it would not have been much fun if the bus had broken down. On another occasion we went for a short camel trek into the Sinai desert. Again, it was a great experience, but when on the way back the boy in charge of my camel proudly informed me in broken English that this camel was called Michael Jackson, any slight tendency I may have had to romanticize the occasion evaporated completely; there seemed no escape from the trappings of Western culture.

Even if we have not encountered actual desert places, we may be familiar with desert experiences. There can be periods in our lives when there is little that is life-giving, and just existing can seem like hard work. We may long for companionship or guidance, but cannot find it. Life may be dominated by coping with things that we find difficult. We may long for God, yet feel that even God is absent. Such things can all make our days feel like a desert experience: barren and lacking in sustenance. Why then is it that over and over again some of the most significant moments in the encounter between human beings and God have their roots in the wilderness, the place where nothing happens?

Perhaps it is for one very simple reason. In that sort of landscape there are few attractions. Where there is very little to attract our attention elsewhere, we have no choice but to be aware of ourselves. Sometimes when things are stripped away from us, space is made for something new. Isaiah is not alone in being convinced that the wilderness would be the place where God would make his glory known – as he had done to Moses and his people at Sinai. This is why he goes on:

> A highway shall be there,
> and it shall be called the Holy Way;
> the unclean shall not travel on it,
> but it shall be for God's people;
> no traveller, not even fools, shall go astray.
> No lion shall be there,
> nor shall any ravenous beast come up on it;
> they shall not be found there,
> but the redeemed shall walk there.
> And the ransomed of the LORD shall return,
> and come to Zion with singing;
> everlasting joy shall be upon their heads;
> they shall obtain joy and gladness,
> and sorrow and sighing shall flee away.
>
> (Isaiah 35.8–10)

I suggest that 'God making his glory known' is a good summary for what Advent is all about. It sounds great – what a wonderful thing to experience! It will not be an easy journey though. This is not about things that are 'nice'. The use of wilderness imagery in Advent suggests that the Advent experience can take us through uncomfortable places. Here we can be more than usually aware of our own weaknesses, with a God who can be quite terrifying. This wilderness is not bland or benign: the sand burns, the land thirsts, the jackals search for prey. These features are paralleled by the things that can blight human life: the inability to see, to hear or to move around easily.

And yet in the final verses, landscape and human life come together not in opposition but in unity. In this formerly hostile environment there is now a clear way to Zion, the focal point of the presence of God with his people. As the poem ends, it is not with a Disney-style sunset drawn with soft edges and a rosy glow; this is the full blaze of the midday sun, where there are no shadows, and everything is seen for what it truly is.

2 December:
Snow, Santa and sleigh bells

Dashing through the snow,
In a one-horse open sleigh,
O'er the fields we go,
Laughing all the way;
Bells on bob-tails ring,
Making spirits bright,
What fun it is to laugh and sing
A sleighing song tonight.

Oh, jingle bells, jingle bells,
Jingle all the way:
Oh, what fun it is to ride
In a one-horse open sleigh.
Jingle bells, jingle bells,
Jingle all the way:
Oh, what fun it is to ride
In a one-horse open sleigh.
(James Lord Pierpont, 1822–93)

Along with Irving Berlin's 'White Christmas', 'Merry Christmas everybody' by Slade, and 'Santa Claus is coming to town' (Coots and Gillespie), this must be one of the songs I hear most often at Christmas. It is so familiar that I could sing along without a thought. It is not that I choose to listen to these things though; they assail my ears every time I enter a shop.

I think I should pause just for a moment, and give warning that I am about to rant (not very reflective, I know, but possibly very therapeutic). If anyone reading this has anything of the cynical 'grumpy old woman' or 'grumpy old man' in them, then please join in. If not, skip to the next paragraph. You see, there are so many things about Christmas as I experience it that make me want to shout at least once every December (if not before), and they tend to come together in the kind of music that is played repeatedly in shopping centres and supermarkets. I know that these songs are fairly frothy and frivolous, and I should not be a killjoy. However, over-familiarity means that my initial attempts at good-natured tolerance quickly fail and my critical voice takes over.

Take 'Jingle bells'. This is a good example of a song that has been hijacked by a particular image of Christmas. It was written in 1850, originally for the Thanksgiving celebration in America. Thought to have been inspired by the sleigh races that took place in the author's home town, it is, as the verses that we never sing go on to show, about the fun and misfortunes of a young man out on the snow in a sleigh. However, it encapsulates a cluster of things that make 'Christmas' a very saleable product: snow, fun, a sleigh, and bells. Even though this sleigh is pulled by a horse, it needs only the tiniest hop in the mind to think of reindeer, then Rudolph, then Santa/Father Christmas. We have a potent image here, which is ruthlessly exploited.

'White Christmas' works in a similar way. It is a sentimental fiction that looks back to an idealized past experience of Christmas – snow, sleigh bells, glistening trees, brightness and feelings of merriment. It tugs on the heartstrings, making us think, 'Wouldn't it be wonderful if . . .' – but it looks backwards, not forwards. The danger is that the picture builds up like a shining bubble, but when the bubble bursts, what is the reality that is left? One very obvious reality is that if you live in the tropics or most of the southern hemisphere, snow will *never* be part of your Christmas celebrations.

It is easy to become critical of this secular and commercially driven version of Christmas. Yet at the same time I am aware of colluding with the anticipation of Christmas. I continue to plan what we are going to do, how we will fit in seeing the various sides of the family, who we can get together without sparks flying, when we are going to make various items of food, what we need to buy, when we will get the presents wrapped up, what we will wear for the work's Christmas festivities, whether we are going to get involved in the school Christmas fair/nativity play/'winter event' and so on. The difficulty is: How do we remain holy in the midst of all this?

If we can set aside any negative feelings we may have, it is much easier to see the tremendous goodness that comes about at Christmas even where there may be no acknowledgement of God. There may be no celebration of the birth of Jesus, but there are extensive expressions of love, demonstrations of generosity, and of inclusion. People put themselves out for others in many different ways – for family, for instance, for those remaining in hospital, for the homeless, and for those with nowhere to go. At the same time, though, there will be those for whom Christmas is purely about commercial gain, or for whom it is an opportunity for indulgence, or for whom there is such pain that there is nothing to celebrate.

Perhaps the real challenge of Advent is that the looming Christmas festivities bring into sharp focus the difficulties we live with all the time. We are constantly faced with an ideal picture, which rarely matches the reality of our experience. Idolatry is the perversion of something that is good. In this very mixed world in which we are immersed, it is not always easy to hang on to the reality of the goodness and presence of God. It is easy to slip into something that is idolatrous – putting something that may well be fundamentally good in the place of God, such that we can no longer see him or hear him.

I will hold on to (and revisit) one image which stands out as an antidote to the Christmas shopping experience I mention above. In November 2010 a video was posted on YouTube entitled 'Christmas Food Court Flash Mob, Hallelujah Chorus'. In the middle of an American shopping centre, as people sat and ate lunch, a young woman with a mobile phone stood up and sang the opening words of the Hallelujah chorus from the *Messiah*. Other people gradually stood and joined in, and after a while it was clear that in among the shoppers was a choir who had prepared the event. They were dressed in ordinary clothes, as people who might work there or be shopping there. It was not entirely clear whether all who stood up were choir members, or were simply joining in, or wanted to show their respect for what was being expressed. Not everyone listened, but many did. The surprise and enjoyment on their faces was evident. Some stood up to record the event on their mobile phones. In the midst of the most secular expression of Christmas were proclaimed the words 'King of kings, and Lord of lords . . . and he shall reign for ever and ever'.

Rather than snow and sleigh bells, it is this picture which will stay in my mind in the period of Advent. We are an embedded people. We are firmly fixed in the midst of a tremendously diverse and often messy world. Wherever we are, what is the song that we want those around us to hear?

3 December: Heaven

Therefore with angels and archangels,
and with all the company of heaven,
we proclaim your great and glorious name,
for ever praising you and saying:

Holy, holy, holy Lord,
God of power and might,
heaven and earth are full of your glory.
Hosanna in the highest.
> (Holy Communion Order One,
> Eucharistic Prayer A, *Common Worship*)

Angels, cherubs, white fluffy clouds, harps and pearly gates: all these are part of our stock of popular images attached to the idea of heaven. We might find them on greetings cards, or in cartoon drawings. Yet what we really think about heaven is a question which might only strike home when we are coming to terms in some way with death. When faced with the end of what we know, the question naturally arises: What happens next?

Along with the images, there are some common ideas about heaven. 'Freedom from pain', 'an end to suffering' and 'being with God' are all important things which are often said when someone dies. Different again is our everyday speech. The word 'heavenly' is commonly used to describe the best possible experience of something, and 'the heavens' often refers simply to the sky above. Whatever we believe, enmeshed in our language are ideas about heaven being the best and somehow 'up there' above us as we go about our daily lives.

There is a wonderful description of heaven in the final chapter of Julian Barnes's novel, *A History of the World in 10½ Chapters*. The narrator finds himself in a situation where he can choose to experience anything he likes. Whether it is breakfast in bed, shopping, sex or golf, it is all wonderful. Time passes, but has little meaning. Anything he wants can be arranged, so when he realizes that he would quite like an assessment of his life – what he can only describe as judgement – this takes place. Yet when the verdict is simply that he is 'OK', it seems rather disappointing. His anxieties, when they surface, rest in the fact that his experience does not match his preconceived idea of heaven. Specifically, he wonders where God is. He asks Margaret, who is assigned to look after him and to whom he can take his queries. Her answer turns the question on its head: Do you want God?

Margaret's answer gets to the heart of this description of a heaven which is almost entirely individualistic. The understanding of free will is exactly this, that you can do what you want when you want with little concern for how it affects other people (we are never told about that). It is about being able to achieve perfection in everything. It is about there being no obligation to do anything at all. Life here is endless in the sense that it really does go on millennium after millennium. There is no sense of tiredness or of ageing. The only things that do not last are things which involve the logical impossibility of being something other than oneself. As the narrator learns, eventually everyone there will make the decision to die off. The final act of free will is to make that choice: to finally and completely cease to exist.

Barnes is entertaining and provocative. He presents us with a picture of what heavenly life might be like if we take seriously some of the popular ideas mentioned above. In considering what we really think about heaven, I want to focus on three things missing from his 'account': transcendence, transformation, and the nature of eternal life.

First, transcendence: the fact that we might say 'the heavens' as a literal way of referring to the sky, reflects this sense we have of heaven being in some way transcendent. It suggests something that rises above mundane human life, something that is not limited by time and place in the same way that we are. There is no sense of this at all in the heaven described by Barnes's narrator. He encounters things which are familiar from his previous experience; just better. In contrast, the quotation at the start of this chapter, taken from the Communion service, picks up on imagery we find in Isaiah's call vision and in the book of Revelation (Isaiah 6.3; Revelation 4.8). In these passages the individuals concerned find themselves witnessing a life which is not part of ordinary human experience. Here, where there are no barriers to the presence of God, the response of the heavenly beings is to proclaim God's holiness and glory.

Second, transformation. Both Isaiah and John (in Revelation) are transformed by visions of transcendence. Isaiah's self-understanding is transformed by his encounter with heavenly reality. He becomes aware of his own shortcomings, yet the action of the heavenly beings is one of cleansing. Isaiah is changed by the experience and enabled to respond to God's call. In Revelation, John is caught up in what is going on. The reality of what he witnesses in this heavenly realm has an impact on his ministry on earth, primarily through what he is told to write. For Barnes's narrator, there is no transformation, only the increased ability to do things in the best possible way; but this is far from what Christian writers mean by transformation.

Third, eternal life. One of the things that Barnes's chapter illustrates is the impossibility of writing about something which is beyond the bounds of our experience. He describes heaven in terms of what we already know. Perhaps it also illustrates the easy misconception of heaven as something that is chrono-logical – the next thing after death. His description is of endless life, not eternal life. Biblical writers portray something rather different. They write much more about encountering the presence of God in the reality of human experience. Isaiah's vision in the Temple, and John's on Patmos, are of a reality which is ever present, if not always visible to the human eye. Such visions are often for specific purposes at specific times, giving us a glimpse of an ever-present reality. The fullness of this reality is what we will experience beyond death.

As a student I heard a talk on prayer in which the speaker described visiting a country church in his work as a bishop. After making his way through a near empty building to the vestry, he was greeted by the vicar, who apologized that the church was so empty of worshippers. 'Oh, it was packed when I came through', was the response of the bishop. More than anything else, this has conveyed to me the reality that we worship not alone, but 'with angels and archangels, and with all the company of heaven'.

4 December: Hell

And the fifth angel blew his trumpet, and I saw a star that had fallen from heaven to earth, and he was given the key to the shaft of the bottomless pit; he opened the shaft of the bottomless pit, and from the shaft rose smoke like the smoke of a great furnace, and the sun and the air were darkened with the smoke from the shaft.

(Revelation 9.1–2)

Given that the imagery of hell is so vivid, it is surprising how little there is that we can say about it with any certainty. The same words and pictures repeatedly fill our imaginations and find their way into film and theatre, books and comics: bottomless pits, fiery furnaces, sulphurous smoke, heat, dark, pain, punishment, eternal torment. Those in charge are devils and demons, dark creatures with horns and tails who perpetrate mischievous or evil deeds. Medieval and early Renaissance literature and art are full of such pictures. Above all, the detailed depiction of hell by Dante in the 'Inferno', the first book of his *Divine Comedy*, has fuelled the imagination of writers ever since.

References to hell as a place permeate both English language and literature. In the plays of Shakespeare, for example, the Ghost of Hamlet's father warns that soon he must go back 'to sulph'rous and tormenting flames' (Act 1, scene 5, line 3). In the twentieth century, C. S. Lewis drew on such imagery in *The Screwtape Letters*, with references to 'our Father Below'. More recently the radio comedy *Old Harry's Game* by Andy Hamilton has exploited the image with comic effect. Hell has captured our imaginations as a place with particular physical features. Yet for all the paper, paint and ink spent on it over hundreds of years, there is little to be sure of. We will not find it on a map. This is not about geography but about something else. Given that the season of Advent has lent itself to a consideration of hell, we need to look at these images. Why are they there, and what do they mean?

As is evident from the words quoted at the start of this chapter from the book of Revelation, the Bible too has its fair share of such vivid imagery. We can see immediately the kind of pictures that fuelled Dante's portrayal of hell and influenced many other writers and artists. Such imagery is, however, concentrated in a fairly small body of literature. In much of the Hebrew Bible it is Sheol that is spoken of as the place of the dead. There is no detailed description, but a sense that this was a rather grey place of inactivity and rest. It is in the later literature of the Hebrew Bible that the more dynamic and vivid images are to be found, specifically within what we know of as apocalyptic literature. Phenomena such as fire, earthquakes, the darkening of the sun and the moon turning to blood, as in the book of Joel (Joel 2.2, 3, 10), are all disruptions in the human sphere – disruptions which are indications of the judgement of God on the wrongdoing of the people. Similar features are described in the books of Ezekiel (for example, Ezekiel 34.12) and Daniel, along with other characteristics of apocalyptic writing, such as visions, angelic interpreters, elaborate descriptions of heaven, and the idea that earthly events have their heavenly counterparts. All of these continued to develop in the writing of the inter-testamental period. In the New Testament, they are particularly evident in the book of Revelation.

In the example that we have from Revelation, the bottomless pit is an idea which comes from the creation mythology prevalent in Canaan and Babylonia when the biblical writers were at work. This mythology presented the creation of the world as the result of a battle between gods. In the Babylonian creation myth, the god Marduk was the god of light and order, and the goddess Tiamat the goddess of evil and chaos. In the battle, Marduk slew Tiamat and split her body in half, using half for the creation of the earth and half for the heavens. Similar ideas were evident in the Canaanite mythology, where the monster Leviathan (or Lotan) was representative of evil or chaos. To say that the biblical writers make use of this imagery is not to suggest that they had nothing better to say. On the contrary, by reworking the images in the way they do, they make a strong theological point about the nature of the one true God. This God, portrayed so powerfully in Genesis 1, is the God who brings order out of chaos.

This biblical vision of creation, however, is not one of a 'sealed universe' in which there is one place for the orderly and good, and one place for the chaotic and bad, with nothing in between. It is not quite so simple. The high point of the created universe as depicted in Genesis 1 is the creation of human beings in the image of God. It is clear from the start that people are given a considerable degree of freedom – and the arena in which that freedom is exercised is the created world. Freedom means that there is always the possibility of chaos disrupting the desired ordering of earthly life.

Inevitably, this is a lightning tour through some big ideas, each one of which really deserves further exploration. Yet there are two particular points which stand out. The first is that wherever we look, the biblical writers never talk about anything more than heaven and earth. As a separate place, hell is never mentioned. If we read the verses that follow Revelation 9.1–2, we find that John goes on to describe the locusts that emerge from the smoke: they have a human face, and the destruction that they are permitted to carry out takes place on the earth, among human beings.

That leads into the second point. The images used are all rooted in the experiences of human life. These features of our physical environment provide us with ways of talking about the less visible and less tangible aspects of life. Jesus offers a perfect example. When reading Mark 9.42–48 in English, we find him referring to 'hell' three times. However, the word he uses, which is often translated as 'hell', is the Greek word *gehenna*. This was the name for the rubbish heap just outside the old city of Jerusalem. Just as he does in his parables, Jesus was using the imagery of the familiar to reinforce his point about current human behaviour.

So where does that leave us? It is easy to see where we get our imagery from when we think about hell, but it is a complete mistake to see these things as relating to actualities, to predictions of specific things. Where apocalyptic imagery is used, the writers are asserting the authority and power of God within this created sphere. Using the imagery which already exists and is understood, biblical writers can talk about living with the reality of evil in the midst of the people, without naming specific rulers or political regimes. If talk of hell is about the reality of evil, then thinking about how we resist it and shrink its sphere of influence is entirely appropriate – not only in Advent, but each day of our lives.

Talk of hell is a way of saying something important about what happens when we die. It may be that we can say nothing more concrete than did the ancient Israelites when they spoke of Sheol. What this language does do is persistently point out that the experience of evil is real, and that people can become so wrapped up in a way of doing things that is contrary to the will of God that they choose never to turn to God. The image of God is so obscured, so deeply hidden, so undernourished and unable to thrive, that when we no longer experience the limitation of human life, the choice of exclusion from the presence of God has already been made. Perhaps that bit of us which would enable life to go on in greater fullness is simply extinguished.

Perhaps it is like being invited to a party, but choosing to stay out in the cold, where you are faced with the consequences of your choice.

5 December: Death

Your hands fashioned and made me;
and now you turn and destroy me.
Remember that you fashioned me like clay;
and will you turn me to dust again?
Did you not pour me out like milk
and curdle me like cheese?
You clothed me with skin and flesh,
and knit me together with bones and sinews.
You have granted me life and steadfast love,
and your care has preserved my spirit.

(Job 10.8–12)

It may be rather odd to focus on what it means to be human in a reflection on death. Death is a subject which continually fascinates us. Yet whatever else there may be to say, we can never get away from the fact that as human beings we will experience the death of others and we will die. Thinking about death therefore forces us to face the limits of our humanity. It faces us with a host of seemingly contradictory ideas. Is death good and natural, or bad and always untimely? Is it grim, or is it beautiful? Is it better to try to control it, or to put up with the suffering?

Death has been romanticized and glorified, its brutality unspoken. It has been dressed up as grim and fearful, for example in the popular image of 'Death the reaper', with black cloak, hooded face and a large scythe. It has sometimes been presented with a moral imperative. The ghost of Jacob Marley visiting Scrooge with clanking chains and deathly demeanour is a vivid illustration of this. In *A Christmas Carol*, Dickens brings Marley to Scrooge as one stuck in death, a warning from beyond the grave of what might happen to Scrooge too if he does not change his ways. Alternatively, however, the character of Death in one of the medieval mystery plays describes himself as the messenger of God. As he has been sent to deal with Herod following the slaughter of the baby boys, the audience are clearly expected to be on the side of Death. The moral aspect of death then includes not only dire warning but the promise of justice. A further image is quite different. When death comes to Julia Garnet at the end of *Miss Garnet's Angel*, Salley Vickers describes a natural stepping forward towards the next thing. What that thing is she does not say, but the mood is one of delight and eagerness.

It would be easy to go on, but that would be to pass beyond the scope of this reflection. There is more to be said about death in the context of Christian theology, and some of it will be said as we reflect on other words later in this book. What we think about death will depend on all sorts of things, not least our experience, and it may well change at different times in our lives. Here, though, we stay with the fact of death as one of the 'four last things' traditionally focused on in Advent. There is a sense in which each of the four – Heaven, Hell, Death and Judgement – are about facing the limits of human life, and that is what Job is doing here.

If there were a film of the creation story from Genesis 2, then Job would be standing in front of it, pointing a finger at it for evidence, and challenging God about what is going on. Job knows that there is no direct link between anything he has done and his suffering. He also knows that God is a fundamental part of life. His words encapsulate the uneasy relationship we have with our humanity. On the one hand, he affirms the wonder of being a human person crafted by God. There is a powerful sense of tender care for the individual, care which clothes the naked and vulnerable. Just as a parent dresses a newborn baby, so Job is 'clothed' with skin, bone and sinew. Job knows that this is part of the capacity to love which is central to human life. Being human means life lived in relationship with this creator God, whose care extends beyond the physical components of life. Whereas a mechanic might admire something he or she has made for its complexity or functionality, God not only cares for but also animates the whole thing. God loves and generates love. On the other hand, however, all is not well. Job paints a picture of something being very wrong. Facing his creator, he suggests that the process is being reversed. He feels that he is being destroyed, reverting to the dust from whence he came. At the same time as declaring the wonder of being a living human being, Job expresses its frailty and fragility.

Lying in the background to all of this are the words of Genesis 2.7: 'Then the LORD God formed man from the dust of the ground, and breathed into his nostrils the breath of life; and the man became a living being.' We are 'dusty' people, earthbound beings. From the moment we are born we have to contend with illness and with bits of us going wrong. Sometimes this can be mended; sometimes not. Bury us and we decay; burn us and there remains a handful of dust. That is what a human person is. Yet it is not the whole story. I vividly remember the first time I saw a dead body. I was struck by the powerful sense of absence. If it sounds contradictory, that is because that is how it felt. It continues to be true: I can see the dead body of a familiar figure and still be struck by the sheer 'not-there-ness' of the person I knew. That may not be good English, but it conveys the experience. To stand with such an awareness of absence is to face the finality and frailty of life as we know it in human form.

Death

When John Donne wrote his 'Devotions upon Emergent Occasions', like Job he was suffering physical illness. Bedridden, and with that same awareness that we are all subject to decay, he heard the tolling of the passing bell at a nearby church announcing the death of an unidentified neighbour. Aware that his own death might be near, he had a strong sense of all human frailty. We are all made from and are part of the same stuff, so 'any man's death diminishes me, because I am involved in mankind, and therefore never send to know for whom the bell tolls; it tolls for thee'.

6 December: Judgement

Almighty God,
give us grace to cast away the works of darkness
and to put on the armour of light,
now in the time of this mortal life,
in which your Son Jesus Christ came to us in
   great humility;
that on the last day,
when he shall come again in his glorious majesty
   to judge the living and the dead,
we may rise to the life immortal;
through him who is alive and reigns with you,
in the unity of the Holy Spirit,
one God, now and for ever.

(The Collect for the First Sunday
of Advent, Common Worship)

A few years ago, a medieval 'Doom' painting was uncovered on the wall above the nave of Holy Trinity Church, Coventry. Like others of its kind, it depicts the Last Judgement scene evoked by Jesus in his parable at the end of Matthew 25. In the painting Jesus is seated in the centre, with the disciples on either side. Mary and John the Baptist kneel in front of him, and on each side human figures clamber from their graves. Some are led up the steps to the gate of heaven on Jesus' right, and others are sent to his left, down towards the fearsome jaws of hell. Painted in the 1430s, it reminded the people of Coventry that a final destination awaited them beyond death, and the decision about where they went was not in their hands. If this painting was designed to instil fear in the hearts of the medieval viewers, it did its job well. I would have been quaking in my boots.

I'm not quaking though – even if it is hard not to think of these 'four last things' as seeking exactly that response. I do not believe for a moment that Christian faith operates on the basis of fear. On the contrary, its basis is love – which careful attention to both the painting and the prayer quoted above makes clear.

Like Jesus' parable and the medieval painting, the Advent collect employs dramatically contrasting imagery. Darkness and light, humility and majesty, mortality and immortality combine to present us with what is now, and the possibility of what might be. It is not a static image that faces us, however, but one of action – our action and God's. The phrase 'works of darkness' suggests active involvement in the darker things of life. This is contrasted with the 'armour of light', which again suggests activity. Although nowadays we might see armour on display during visits to stately homes or castles, hundreds of years ago you bought it because you were willing to use it. As we shall see in Southwell's poetry, armour reminds us that living out the ways of Christ involves battling with things that are in conflict with what he desires for us. The prayer makes it clear that we do not do this alone, however. Jesus 'came to us', evidence of the movement of God in love towards us. It is only through this movement into the darkness of the world that Jesus is experienced in majesty, and it is only through this action of humility that he has any role as judge.

I do not like the word 'judgement'. I do not like the ideas that it suggests to me – at least at first. Perhaps I have watched too many courtroom dramas on television, but there is at least a grain of reality reflected in them. In British crown courts we will still find the judge seated higher up and a little apart from the other participants. It is still the case that the high court judge will normally appear dressed in robes and a wig. As on television, a courtroom is an austere scene, where defendants and victims, witnesses, barristers and solicitors, jury and clerks each have their proper place and are kept there. It has to do with something bad having been done, with the truth being exposed and punishment handed out. In a televised murder trial set before the abolition of the death penalty, even though we know we are watching fiction, it is nevertheless a chilling moment when the judge places the black cap on his head and the sentence of death is passed. That is it. No more chances.

When I hear the word 'judgement', it is this sort of thing that first comes to mind. There is a lurking fear of being found out. I'm never really sure what I might be found out for. I think 'judgement' conjures up a vague idea that when it is my turn, some sort of angelic secretary will present God with a list of all the trivial misdemeanours I have ever committed. Actually, I think that God has much more important things to be concerned about. Above all, though, that sort of idea leaves no room for the whole business of forgiveness. No. We need to remember that judgement is not necessarily negative. It is not always a condemnation of what is bad but can be a great affirmation of what is good.

It is worth pointing out that in ordinary daily life we make judgements all the time. We see other people's behaviour and make decisions about their motives. Without having to think terribly hard, we make decisions about what is good and what is not. Teachers will frequently make positive judgements about their pupils' progress or pieces of work. We see what helps our children to thrive, and what puts up barriers to that happening. The things that have become law are nearly always derived from decisions of this kind. Our laws reflect the desire so to order our lives that people may thrive, and things that cause damage have no place. It is a natural extension of this to see God as being the one who can help sort out the rather messy world we live in. As we saw in Isaiah's picture of the wilderness, there is nothing damaging on the highway that emerges in that difficult landscape.

So perhaps judgement is not a scary thing after all, but an expression of God's love for the world he has created. Two features of the Doom painting I mentioned illustrate this. First, the human figures coming out of their graves are naked. There is nothing which can hide us from the presence of God – no fine clothes, no uniforms, nothing which might reflect particular status within the human community. Before God we are all as vulnerable as each other.

Second, we are not the only ones. The word 'vulnerable' comes from the Latin word meaning 'to wound'. As vulnerable human beings we can be wounded. One of the striking things about this particular Doom painting is that the wounds Jesus suffered are clearly visible. Just as the Advent prayer points out, so the painting reminds us that Jesus can only come as Judge because he first came in humility – because he first got so immersed in human life that within it he suffered and died. As the robes and wig are symbols of a judge's authority, so the wounds in his hands and side are symbols of Christ's authority. The Judge is not a distant stranger, but one who has been here too, demonstrating his love for each and every one of us.

'New prince, new pompe' by Robert Southwell (1561–95)

Behold a silly tender babe
   In freezing Winter night
In homely manger trembling lies
   Alas a piteous sight.
The Inns are full, no man will yield
   This little Pilgrim Bed;
But forc'd he is with silly beasts
   In Crib to shroud his head.
Despise him not for lying there
   First what he is enquire;
An orient pearl is often found
   In depth of dirty mire.
Weigh not his Crib, his wooden dish,
   Nor beasts that by him feed;
Weigh not his mother's poor attire,
   Nor Joseph's simple weed.
This stable is a Prince's Court,
   The Crib his chair of state,
The beasts are parcel of his pomp,
   The wooden dish his plate.
The persons in that poor attire
   His royal liveries wear;
The prince himself is come from heaven:
   This pompe is prizèd there.
With joy approach, O Christian wight,
   Do homage to thy King,
And highly prize this humble pomp
   Which he from heaven doth bring.

7 December

Behold a silly tender babe
In freezing Winter night
In homely manger trembling lies
Alas a piteous sight.
The Inns are full, no man will yield
This little Pilgrim Bed;
But forc'd he is with silly beasts
In Crib to shroud his head.

So – we've finally arrived. Seven days into December and at last we are at the nativity scene, described here by Robert Southwell. His words clearly appealed to Benjamin Britten, who set them to music in *A Ceremony of Carols*. The sense of mystery in Britten's music echoes the invitation Southwell offers to his readers to look again at the well-known scene – 'Behold' is his opening word. That is a very good thing to do – simply to stop, and look. The nativity story will be familiar to us from children's presentations in school or church and from the huge variety of images on Christmas cards – from the cute and cuddly to the beautiful stained-glass window or the detail from a medieval painting. But even if we feel we know it well, it is always good to stop and look. There are always new things to notice. Here, Southwell paints a picture with words, and invites us to look with him at what he sees.

It might be an idea to pause here, with this 'Behold', and remind ourselves of what we know of the birth of Jesus and the manger. The answer is really not very much. Both Matthew and Luke describe Jesus' birth in the opening chapters of their Gospels. Matthew mentions Bethlehem but nothing at all about the circumstances of the birth or the kind of house in which it took place (chapter 2). The only specific mention of a manger comes in Luke 2.1–20, where the reason for the journey to Bethlehem and the visit of the shepherds are also mentioned. Perhaps this is a good time to read Matthew's and Luke's accounts again – it can be something of a challenge at times to stay with the story and simply see what is there.

In these opening lines of 'New prince, new pompe', Southwell chooses words that draw our attention to details of the scene. Some of these words have changed their meanings slightly over the course of the last four hundred years, and unless we know this, their use here may well strike us as odd. That very oddity, however, can help to bring fresh insights on a very familiar scene. I want to highlight four of these words – 'silly', 'tender', 'Pilgrim' and 'shroud'.

Both the baby and the beasts are described as 'silly'. Nowadays we tend to use this word to describe a person or a person's behaviour in a rather disparaging way. It implies that they are foolish, not worth bothering with. While that is not what Southwell means, there is a link. The word can mean 'unintelligent', again, in a rather negative way, but seen from a more positive point of view 'silly' can mean 'simple' or 'innocent'. This is exactly what a baby is, and this one is no different. We may have the benefit of knowing that in some mysterious way this baby is God, but Southwell wants us to pay attention to what we *see*. Here is a baby whose knowledge of the world he is born into extends to the sound, the sight and the feel of his parents, no more. Similarly, this baby is 'tender' – soft, vulnerable, with no defences.

If Southwell wants to remind us of the earthliness of the scene, however, there are also hints of something more. In what sense is this baby a 'Pilgrim'? Again, nowadays this word is always used with religious overtones. A pilgrim is someone who makes a journey to a place of special significance to do with certain important beliefs. In the past, however, the word could simply mean 'a traveller' or 'wayfarer', someone who was a stranger in a place. Certainly Mary and Joseph had just made a journey, albeit one the Roman overlords had required for political not religious reasons. Although not born until after they arrived, one could argue of course that Jesus too made this journey. Later religious writers emphasized the significance of Bethlehem as the destination. It did have theological importance as 'the city of David'. I'm not convinced, however, that it was this journey that Southwell had in mind when describing the baby as 'Pilgrim'. It seems to me that there is a hint of something more here. Could there be a suggestion perhaps of the thought that this child is one who has travelled, one who is welcomed and yet is a visitor, one whose roots are elsewhere?

At the same time as encouraging us simply to notice the scene, the poet hints at the bigger picture. In referring to the child as 'Pilgrim', he expands our horizons in one way. In his use of the word 'shroud', he hints at what is to come. Perhaps there is nothing unusual in this. A shroud is simply a cover, and to shroud something means to cover it. It is hard to read the line, however, without also having in mind the common use of the word to describe the cloth that wraps a dead body prior to burial.

See then this baby, born in impoverished surroundings, for whom bed is a manger and companions are the animals of a stable. See this baby, one who has in some sense travelled far, and whose humanity – like that of us all – is limited by death.

8 December

Despise him not for lying there
First what he is enquire;
An orient pearl is often found
In depth of dirty mire.

Good poets don't beat about the bush. One of the appealing things about Southwell is that at the same time as conjuring up vivid images of a scene, he is also quite directive when it comes to involving his audience. From the opening exhortation to look, we are now directed to consider how we feel about what we see.

The more familiar a text is, the harder it can be to stay with it and allow something to strike us. I find I tend to skate over the first two lines here and focus on the image of the pearl. After all, don't we know what we are looking at – a baby? Yet Southwell does not want us to get away with making assumptions, and reinforces his point with the image of a deep and dirty mire. These lines contrast something most precious and beautiful with the dirt and muck of a stable. By alluding to the buried pearl, they challenge us to consider our attitude to poverty, and to reflect on what we value.

Robert Southwell was a deeply religious man who was steeped in the language and imagery of the Bible. Here he draws together two of Jesus' parables of hidden treasure.

The kingdom of heaven is like treasure hidden in a field, which someone found and hid; then in his joy he goes and sells all that he has and buys that field.

Again, the kingdom of heaven is like a merchant in search of fine pearls; on finding one pearl of great value, he went and sold all that he had and bought it.

(Matthew 13.44–46)

Each of these vignettes requires that we engage our imagination. Imagine being the person who finds the treasure. Imagine the moment of discovery, followed by the need to decide what to do. How can you acquire this honestly? Imagine covering it over again, and the process of selling everything you own. How do you feel when your possessions have all gone? How do you feel when you can go and buy the field, so that the treasure can be yours?

What about if you were the merchant? Your job has been one of searching; imagine finding the finest specimen you have ever come across. How does that feel? It is very costly. How can you get hold of it? Think of everything that you own. You have to sell it all in order for this pearl to be yours. What must it be worth in order for you to do that?

There's a great deal of risk involved in these stories – recklessness in fact. Surely we should proceed with great caution before imitating these two characters? One of the characteristics of Jesus' storytelling is that he often stretches the boundaries of 'normality', such that we are pushed to think hard about what we believe. Here, as in many other cases, he makes use of contrasts to emphasize his point. The extravagance of the response forces us to ask questions about the value of the treasure and the pearl. Questions about the things that are left out bounce back on to our own situation. How much did they already own, and what exactly did they sell? Were they completely independent or did they have family responsibilities – and if so, what did their families think?

There's one more thing to note before we leave these stories and go back to Southwell, and that concerns the kingdom of heaven itself. Although the parables seem very similar, Jesus is actually pointing out two different things here. In the first vignette, he says that the kingdom of heaven is like a static object – it is like the treasure, something marvellous and of great value that is to be discovered. That is probably a familiar idea. The second image, however, is more teasing: the kingdom of heaven is not said to be like the pearl; it is like the merchant. It is not simply about some thing or place we want to get to, but is also about the way we behave. Living in the kingdom of heaven, the place of God's reign, involves the kind of reckless-ness and extravagance Jesus portrays in his stories. It is not about staying with what looks safe, secure and sensible. It is about taking risks – and they start with the risk of vision that Southwell is talking about.

Returning to the poem, it is not surprising that we find some of the same characteristics. Again, a sharp contrast is drawn. Southwell draws a contrast between a fine pearl of the eastern seas and a baby bedded among animals, and therefore of very low social status. To possess a pearl – as nowadays perhaps – was to be able to demonstrate to others one's wealth and social standing. To have no home or security speaks for itself. Southwell implies that people in such a state would have been looked down on as a matter of course. Perhaps it was thought that such poverty was their own fault. At any rate, they were clearly of no use; only people and things which had power and influence were worth attending to.

Having drawn our eyes to the scene, Southwell now wants us not to dismiss it but to ask what it is about. By pointing us to Jesus' stories, he challenges us to think about what we value. More than that, though, he challenges us to look in a different way at what we see. He wants us to be willing to go deeper, to see beyond the superficial, to find what might be buried. This – not surprisingly – involves risk. It is, however, a qualified risk. It is the risk of attuning your will to God's will for you. It is about seeing things the way God sees, and looking at things from God's perspective.

9 December

Weigh not his Crib, his wooden dish,
    Nor beasts that by him feed;
Weigh not his mother's poor attire,
    Nor Joseph's simple weed.
This stable is a Prince's Court,
    The Crib his chair of state,
The beasts are parcel of his pomp,
    The wooden dish his plate.
The persons in that poor attire
    His royal liveries wear;
The prince himself is come from heaven:
    This pompe is prizèd there.

Most popular images of the nativity that we see at Christmas do not portray any sense of the reality of the situation. They are often stylized: the cute and appealing, the pious, the loving mother and so on. Perhaps the stable had just been cleaned out, yet even the shepherds rarely have mud on their feet. It doesn't take much imagination, however, to realize that it would probably have been cold, quite dark, smelly, and not clean by today's standards. Health and safety inspectors looking at this place of birth would have found plenty to comment on. Perhaps that is just the point: whether we are reading or looking, we do so from our own point of view and from our own particular circumstances.

Well of course we do – but the challenge here is not to stop with that. We do sometimes refuse to see what is unwelcome.

We tend to keep the dust and dirt and pain and rejection out of the nativity images because Christmas is a nice, warm, happy time when we don't want to have to think about such things – is it not? For many of us, it is easy to make Christmas into a form of escapism. We often want to be distracted from the difficulties life brings, and to have a break, just for a while.

It's a bit of an about-turn, then, to have to recognize that this scene is what God has chosen. This is God's very particular way of doing things. This set of circumstances is not just a convenient disguise; it is a positive choice. The cold is really cold, the pain of birth is real, the anguished debates about parenthood are truly heart-searching. When faced with God's choice, how do we feel about our choices?

It is very easy to make quick judgements. Most of us do it all the time. We make decisions about people on the basis of how they dress, where they live, what they possess, what they do for a living, where they send their children to school and so on. We often laugh at these attitudes when the contrasts between people are exploited and exaggerated for comic effect on television. Depending on age, of course, you might have seen this in the likes of *The Good Life*, *To the Manor Born* or *Keeping up Appearances*. More recently the way we tend to stereotype other people is exploited for humour in programmes such as *Little Britain* and *Come Fly With Me*. However, what these rarely do – for it would spoil the effect – is go deeper. We are not invited to consider why people might do what they do; we are given just enough information for the comedy to work. When applied to real life, however, the effects of such quick judgements can become divisive. One person's apparent oddity may in fact be evidence of how well he or she is managing after a period of mental illness. Another may be struggling with chronic or terminal illness. Another may be coming to terms with death or divorce – or any number of things which no one should feel under pressure to have to explain widely.

Southwell asks us to 'weigh not' the appearance of what we see. We might speak of giving weight to something – in other words, attaching importance to it. It is the same meaning here. Southwell asks us not to give weight to how things look when we gaze at the scene in the stable, but to see it in a different way. Again, he makes use of contrasts to emphasize his point. Yes, there is a manger, there are wooden utensils, poor and simple clothing – but look at these in terms of the royal court, the highest human authority in the land. Here you are looking at the court of a prince, you are looking at the throne or chair of state, you are looking at attendants dressed in the chosen clothes of the prince they serve, you are looking at the prince himself. God affirms this humanity by choosing it. This is where God chooses to be. More than that, though, this earthly stuff is valued in heaven. This is no reluctant choice but a whole-hearted embracing of humanity as it is.

If we are in a position to understand the reasoning behind the choices people make about the way they live, we can find ourselves surprised, and our sympathy engaged. Sometimes, however, we simply have to suspend our tendency to judge or to jump to quick conclusions, and let something be. Sometimes we have to ask God for help in seeing things from a different point of view. Sometimes we find that the values of heaven then have a bigger space in which to grow. Something like this was in the mind of the author of Hebrews, whose readers are urged: 'Let mutual love continue. Do not neglect to show hospitality to strangers, for by doing that some have entertained angels without knowing it' (Hebrews 13.1–2).

10 December

> With joy approach, O Christian wight,
>> Do homage to thy King,
> And highly prize this humble pomp
>> Which he from heaven doth bring.

How often do you find yourself talking to someone about 'doing homage'? Probably not often – if ever. I don't suppose that the word 'allegiance' comes up very often either. Yet the question of who or what has authority over us is perhaps a bit closer to home. All these ideas are woven together in the image Southwell presents us with in these last four lines of 'New prince, new pompe'.

Imagine for a moment what life would have been like for you had you lived in Britain about six hundred years ago. Perhaps you would have been involved in the manufacture of cloth, in farming or even in education. Like very many women, perhaps you would have been occupied with the business of raising your own family, caring for three generations. You might have been involved in service in the household of the local gentry – in the best rooms, in the kitchens, in the stables or as a tenant on their farmland and so on. You might have been one of the gentry, actively employed in the service of the monarch or expected to present yourself well at the court of the king and queen.

There are many possibilities, but one thing would be very different: far fewer of us would have owned our own homes or any land or any significant property. Whole communities would have been dependent on their local landowner for their livelihood. In some cases this would have been an abbey or monastery rather than the family at the local manor-house. The key thing in your life would have been the relationship you had with whoever you were dependent on, and this would have been a relationship of inequality. Even the most powerful in the land were dependent: they would have been dependent on the king or queen. And those at the very top were dependent on the support of others. The word 'homage' conjures up this world. It is all about who you relate to, where you put your loyalty and to whom you give allegiance. Would you place yourself on the line for your local lord? Would you be willing to give yourself in service to your ruler?

At first glance this may all seem rather remote, but if we stay with these thoughts for even a short time, we find that the same ideas are with us now. We may no longer use the imagery conjured up by Southwell in the word 'homage', but we all live with the daily reality of being under authority. This might be that of more senior members of staff in our place of work, or the authority of an institution as a whole or the political ideas enshrined in law. It might be the authority of a bank: Will it or will it not give us an account or a mortgage? It might simply be a question of where we shop (after all, how many of us carry 'loyalty cards'?).

At the beginning of *The Voyage of the Dawn Treader* by C. S. Lewis, the children Edmund and Lucy are together in Lucy's bedroom in the house where they are staying. Here a picture of a sailing ship hangs on the wall. As they stand in front of it and talk about how like the ships of Narnia she is, they are joined by their obnoxious cousin Eustace, who delights in teasing them about this – to his mind – imaginary place. Yet as they talk the movement of the ship becomes real, their senses are assailed by the smell and feel of the wind and the spray, and they are there – sucked into the water and then pulled up on to the deck, with not a picture frame or bedroom wall in sight. Lucy and Edmund delight in being with old friends, while Eustace is ultimately transformed by the adventures he has there. When they are finally returned to the place they started from, outside Narnia, all are changed by their experiences.

That is a wonderfully vivid illustration of what is going on in this poem. Southwell began by asking us to look. Having drawn us nearer, he closes his poem with the invitation to step forward and enter in. We are to come with joy, and to 'do homage'. In other words, he urges us to be part of the activity he depicts, not pushed from behind but drawn in by what we see. We are back to where we started: What is it that we see? It is in fact a very topsy-turvy world which Southwell urges us to enter. He shows us a young couple and a baby, a long way from home, in a borrowed stable, a temporary resting place. It is all very fragile and provisional. Yet we are asked to come as if we were in the service of a great lord or king. We are to come as those who have little or no wealth, who own no property and have little or no authority or power over others.

With his challenge to see that there is more here than meets the eye, Southwell also challenges us to reconsider where the lines of authority lie in our lives. If you spend a lot of time as a director of a company, a team leader or manager of others, you may find that here, in the presence of the baby in the manger, any perception of your own importance may well have to change. In this relationship, worldly status is important only in that we acknowledge it, but can then set it to one side. Paying homage means putting everything we have in the service of another, into the hands of one who is greater than we are.

Allow yourself to be drawn into the picture. Where would you be?

'The burning babe' by
Robert Southwell (1561–95)

As I in hoary winter's night stood shivering in the
  snow,
Surpris'd I was with sudden heat, which made my
  heart to glow;
And lifting up a fearful eye to view what fire was near,
A pretty babe all burning bright did in the air appear
who scorched with excessive heat such floodes of
  tears did shed –
As though his floodes should quench his flames,
  which with his tears were fed.
'Alas', quoth he, 'but newly born in fiery heates I fry,
Yet none approach to warme their hearts or feel my
  fire but I.
My faultless breast the furnace is, the fuel wounding
  thorns,
Love is the fire and sighs the smoke, the ashes
  shame and scorns,
The fuel, Justice layeth on, and Mercy blows the coals.
The metal in this furnace wrought are men's defiled
  souls,
For which as now on fire I am to work them to
  their good;
So will I melt into a bath to wash them in my
  blood.'
With this he vanished out of sight and swiftly
  shrunk away,
And straight I called unto mind that it was
  Christmas day.

11 December

As I in hoary winter's night stood shivering in the
   snow,
Surpris'd I was with sudden heat, which made my
   heart to glow;
And lifting up a fearful eye to view what fire was near,
A pretty babe all burning bright did in the air appear.

In contrast to 'New prince, new pompe' there is no nativity
scene here. There is a baby, and we are told that it is Christmas
Day, but there the similarity ends. We are not invited to enter
into a familiar scene. We stand as outsiders, looking in on the
poet's experience. Two things stand out in these opening lines:
the strangeness of the vision itself, but also the powerful sense
of aloneness and isolation experienced by the poet.

Southwell describes being outside in the snow on a winter's
night, when anyone might reasonably have liked to be inside
with a roaring fire in the hearth. He does not say whether or
not there was anyone with him, but it seems likely that he was
alone. I find myself wondering what he was thinking, although
he does not tell us that either. Perhaps he had been pondering
the question, What is Christmas Day all about? Perhaps his
concerns were about the more immediate situation of being
a Catholic in Elizabethan England. It was all right if you toed
the line, but if you wanted to assert your right both to remain
a Catholic and be loyal to the Queen, you were likely to get
into trouble. This was a time of continuing religious turmoil,
and in government there was tremendous fear of Catholic plots,
supported by the Catholic courts of Europe, against the Queen.

Southwell's question may have been the familiar, Where is God in all this?

Whatever was in Southwell's mind, what he records is a strange vision. The first awareness of it is not the sight, but the feeling. In that cold and hostile environment there comes a sense of warmth. It is a feeling that meets his need, shivering as he is. Even so, he is understandably a little afraid as he looks to see what on earth can be providing the heat in such a cold and dark place. What he sees is a baby, but it seems to be suspended in the air, and is burning. It could be gruesome, but while the sight is undoubtedly surreal, this is not the stuff of horror movies. Although the meaning of the word 'pretty' has altered a little over time, it is still here a positive thing. The burning baby in the air is in some way pleasing to the eye, with a look of intelligence. More than that, however, to anyone as immersed in biblical literature as Southwell, it is a vision which echoes that of Moses and the burning bush.

Moses was a man on the run. What a dramatic turn his life had taken – more than once. Born a Hebrew, nursed by his mother after an escapade in the river as a baby, he was then raised as royalty, adopted by the Pharaoh's daughter. Yet when we meet him as an adult, we see him at the heart of the oppression under which the Hebrews laboured for the Egyptians. After murdering an Egyptian and failing in his attempt to conceal his crime, he flees for his life. Although he is welcomed into the family of Jethro and settles with a Midianite wife and child, the isolation described at the start of Exodus chapter 3 is more than geographical. The taking of another man's life has cut him off from the places and families of his upbringing, and the fear of consequences prevents him from freely returning. What took him so far through the wilderness that particular day, we do not know. There is no indication that he was looking for anything other than pasture for the flocks. Yet it was out there, away from anyone else, that he was confronted by God in the fire of the bush that burned without being consumed.

The contrast between a Middle Eastern desert roughly three thousand years ago and a winter's night in sixteenth-century England could not be much greater, but in the experience of both men we are on common ground. This is about the way God comes to someone when that person is not looking, when it is least expected, and in the most unexpected place. It is about being in a hostile environment. It is about being in a state of aloneness when it seems that there is nothing left to draw on. Whether imposed or chosen, such circumstances can make us question our fundamental convictions. Who am I? What am I doing here? What is the basis of the way I orient my life?

For Southwell, the answer to these questions meant remaining true to his Catholic faith. Although he continued to assert his loyalty to Queen Elizabeth I, in the climate of fear that governed the politics of the time he was forced to choose. Charged with treason, he was put to death at the age of 34. For Moses, it meant turning back to face the place he had come from, and doing what he never thought he could do. We do not know what he wanted, any more than we know why he was there, but we do know that he did not want this. A powerful meeting with God would be hard enough to cope with at the best of times, but the task he was then given, he tried his hardest to wriggle out of. Not surprisingly God becomes angry, but he does not let Moses off. Exasperated, he offers Aaron as spokesperson.

In that cold and dark place, it seems that Southwell was given a moment of clarity, which he goes on to describe. The poem reflects the conviction that comes from standing alone and remaining true when the world around is indifferent or actively hostile. This is not the conviction of someone assured of his or her own strength. It was unexpected, but given in a situation where there was nothing else to rely on. It is something conveyed by R. S. Thomas in the penultimate poem of *Counterpoint*:

> When we are weak, we are
> strong. When our eyes close
> on the world, then somewhere
> within us the bush
>
> burns. When we are poor
> and aware of the inadequacy
> of our table, it is to that
> uninvited the guest comes.

12 December

And lifting up a fearful eye to view what fire was near,
A pretty babe all burning bright did in the air appear
who scorched with excessive heat such floodes of
    tears did shed –
As though his floodes should quench his flames,
    which with his tears were fed.
'Alas', quoth he, 'but newly born in fiery heates I fry,
Yet none approach to warme their hearts or feel my
    fire but I.'

In most images of the nativity, the baby is the centrepiece. He often appears to be passive, simply lying there as babies do. Any activity in the scene stems from the adults around him. In reading the biblical birth narratives, it is what is said about him that matters; he of course says nothing. In this poem the picture Southwell paints is very different. The baby remains the centre of attention, but here it is he who speaks, and the activity of the flames and tears are centred on him. Having set the scene, the poet recedes while the speaking baby captures our attention. His words reflect the ageless wisdom and knowledge of God's perspective on human life, and yet there remains something childlike. The baby's lament has an element of longing to it. These are not the tears of a child who wants his own way for the sake of it. This is the sorrow of a child who wants others to come and join his game, not because he is too proud to go to them – far from it – but because he knows just how wonderful his game is, and longs for others to know that too.

This sense of the longing of God for his people pervades the Old Testament. It is part of the whole personality of God, which embraces anger and love. These two, often completely separate, are nevertheless very closely associated and frequently found together. Love generates great anxiety when a child is late home, but it is often expressed as anger when the child arrives. In biblical literature, anger is frequently evoked by injustice, and is aimed at those who consistently pursue their own desires rather than those of the giver of life. The reason for Moses' call in Exodus 3 was the longing of God to rescue the Israelites from the dire situation they were in.

The twin themes of anger and love tend to be particularly strong in the words of the prophets. Behind the expression of anger is the longing God has for people to discover just how wonderful life would be if they did things his way – not because God is a despot but because his overwhelming attitude towards the human race is one of love. The despot seeks to control. God seeks to liberate. The prophet Hosea expresses clearly this longing sorrow and love of God for his people. In Hosea 11 this compassion is expressed through powerful images of parental love and care: God carried his people in his arms, taught them to walk, healed them, led them with love and fed them. Although they continue to turn away from him, God will not reject them. It is an image which is echoed in the final lines of Hopkins' sonnet, 'God's Grandeur'. Having asked why people do not attend to God, and lamented the tarnishing effects we often have on the world we live in, he concludes that even so, we are not abandoned:

> Because the Holy Ghost over the bent
> World broods with warm breast and with ah! bright
>   wings.

These are images of light in dark places, flickers of hope, reminders of the greater reality in a world in which God is frequently ignored.

These reflections on Southwell's poem generate a further line of thought. The baby in the vision is both alone and lonely, longing for others to draw near and receive what he has to give. Is it true to say such things of God? I suggest that there is something about the dynamic of aloneness and community experienced by human beings which mirrors the aloneness and community of God. There is of course a difference between being alone and being lonely – they do not always come together. Being alone can be a positive choice, enjoyable and sometimes even a necessary experience, perhaps for a limited time. Being lonely is not positive, and can happen as often among a crowd of people as when actually alone. Loneliness is about a lack of connection with other people; a sense of not being heard, understood, valued or wanted. It might be a familiar idea that God is alone, while the loneliness of God seems strange.

Take the distinction between *being* in love and *falling* in love. Being in love means being able to be vulnerable to another person, willing to let that person see the warts-and-all me. We are able to be like this because we trust that the other person loves us and accepts us as we are – just as we do in return. That is a happy state to be in. Before that, though, is the stage of falling in love. Falling in love and acting on those feelings means taking a risk. It is the risk of being rejected, of finding that the offer of our love is refused. This is not uncommon, but it can feel very lonely. The risk of love means that somewhere in the dynamic of aloneness and community there is always the possibility of loneliness.

This takes us to the heart of the Christian understanding of God as Trinity. One of the most profound images that I have encountered of this is that of three hares chasing each other in a circular dance. This has a Greek name, *perichoresis* – the round dance of the Trinity. Here we see the way in which the love of God permeates the relationships between the identical hares, representing Father, Son and Holy Spirit. We see endlessly reciprocated joy and enjoyment in the dance. Above all, as we watch we are caught up in the dance. In the person of Jesus, the human and divine permeate one another, and we too are embraced by the dynamic love of God.

Of course, not all will enjoy the dance. As Southwell reminds us, the longing of this child who laments the failure of others to draw near is the longing of the God of love for his beloved people.

13 December

—•◦•—

'My faultless breast the furnace is, the fuel wounding
  thorns,
Love is the fire and sighs the smoke, the ashes shame
  and scorns,
The fuel, Justice layeth on, and Mercy blows the coals.
The metal in this furnace wrought are men's defiled
  souls,
For which as now on fire I am to work them to
  their good;
So will I melt into a bath to wash them in my blood.'
With this he vanished out of sight and swiftly
  shrunk away,
And straight I called unto mind that it was Christmas
  day.

One of the extraordinary things about these lines is that with
the exception of the last two, they are spoken by a child – a baby
whose vulnerability has already been made very clear. The image
that is conjured up, however, is not at all compatible with
this. We are not in a quiet stable looking on in adoration, but
in a workshop where through the smelting process metals
are refined to produce their pure form. The furnace blazes, the
air is hot. Through care and expertise, the impure solids are
melted down in extreme temperatures. In its purity, the metal
that results is ready for use. This is the image that Southwell
chooses to dwell on in this Christmas poem. Why?

I have to say that no matter how many times I read this
poem, I always find its imagery strange and uncomfortable.

I wonder how much Southwell's own experience of religious persecution contributed to what he wrote. Being faced with experiences of life which profoundly challenge one's beliefs will have an impact on the way in which those beliefs are expressed. Take the two cathedrals of Guildford and Coventry. They were consecrated only a year apart, in 1961 and 1962, and yet they could not be more different. The decision to build a new cathedral in Guildford was taken in 1928, and building work began in 1935. However, because the work was interrupted by the Second World War, it was not completed for another 26 years. Broadly speaking, it looks as you might expect an English cathedral to look.

In contrast, Coventry's new cathedral does not meet traditional expectations of what a church or cathedral will look like. It exists as a direct result of the destruction of the Blitz in November 1940, and in its design there are clearly things which reflect the fact of that experience of suffering. The echo in the chancel furniture of the cross of nails is one example. The whole of the 'back wall' of the cathedral is a glass window, engraved with angelic figures, through which one looks on to the bombed-out shell of the old cathedral. Its 'strangeness' comes from the experience that gave rise to it.

Perhaps Southwell's experience made him particularly aware of the cost of what God began in the birth of Jesus. For each element of the scene in the workshop there is a corresponding meaning, which the babe explains. The furnace, which contains the fire, is the babe's own breast. It is a reference to his physical body, but Southwell wants to draw our attention to the heart, for the fire that burns in this furnace is Love. There are then two references to the fuel for the fire, which require a little teasing out. First, the babe remarks that the fuel is 'wounding thorns' and, second, that this fuel is laid on by Justice. The 'wounding thorns' remind us of the crown of thorns placed on Jesus' head by the mocking soldiers. Like the babe in the poem, Jesus is seen at that point to be vulnerable. How then can Southwell claim that this fuel is laid on by Justice? Surely such treatment was highly unjust? Here again it is a case of where you stand. From one point of view we can see that soldiers have often been used by governments as instruments of justice. In some circumstances they might be involved in bringing about a just situation by punishing wrongdoing. On the other hand, from the perspective of anyone concerned with humanitarian issues, the soldiers' treatment of Jesus was clearly unjust.

Yet neither of these explanations is satisfactory from a theological point of view. It is one of the paradoxes of Christian faith that this deeply mocking and apparently unjust action was in fact an element of God's justice. The justice of God is about doing what was necessary to transform human nature from its sullied state into what it was always intended to be: a true reflection of the image of God, declared to be 'very good' (Genesis 1.27, 31). This is an action which from a human point of view on the basis of merit alone we do not deserve. But it is Mercy that 'blows the coals': that which brings oxygen and therefore energy to the fire of love is the mercy of God. Hence the image of the crucible in the workshop: it is the place of transformation. In the sighs, shame and scorn of Jesus' crucifixion, 'defiled souls' are purified. Just in case we were in any remaining doubt, the babe's words about his blood complete the image. He is the final piece dissolving in the pot of molten metal, the 'bath' in which we are washed – not only the crucible of his crucifixion and death, but also perhaps an allusion to Holy Communion and the ongoing cleansing of all who come to God in that act of worship.

There is an intensity about all of this which gives way to a slight sense of relief when we reach the last two lines of the poem. The vision evaporates, yet with its absence the aloneness of the poet is emphasized. If there is an element of loneliness in that dynamic between aloneness and community, then Southwell brings it out here. In contrast to many images of the nativity where a variety of people come to see the baby, here we are left with a strong impression of the solitude of God and the aloneness of the believer.

The poem is entitled 'The burning babe', for that is what it describes. The babe uses the imagery of the metalworker's crucible. Yet in him the fire and the worker are one. The child is on fire with Love. Out of the fire of the furnace comes something changed for a new purpose. St Paul would have understood immediately the strangeness of this poem. He wrote to friends at the church in Corinth:

> From now on, therefore, we regard no one from a human point of view; even though we once knew Christ from a human point of view, we know him no longer in that way. So if anyone is in Christ, there is a new creation: everything old has passed away; see, everything has become new!
>
> (2 Corinthians 5.16–17)

'New heaven, new war' by Robert Southwell (1561–95)

Come to your heaven you heavenly choirs –
Earth hath the heaven of your desires.
Remove your dwelling to your god,
A stall is now his best abode.
Sith men their homage do deny
Come Angels all their fault supply.

His chilling cold doth heat require;
Come Seraphims in lieu of fire.
This little ark no cover hath
Let Cherubs' wings his body swath.
Come Raphael, this babe must eat;
Provide our little Toby meat.

Let Gabriel be now his groom
That first took up his earthly room.
Let Michael stand in his defence
Whom love hath link'd to feeble sense.
Let graces rock when he doth cry,
And Angels sing his lullaby.

The same you saw in heavenly seat
Is he that now sucks Mary's teat.
Agnize your king, a mortal wight,
His borrowed weed lets not your sight.
Come kiss the manger where he lies
That is your bliss above the skies.

This little babe so few days old
Is come to rifle Satan's fold.
All hell doth at his presence quake,
Though he himself for cold do shake.

For in this weak unarmed wise,
The gates of hell he will surprise.

With tears he fights and wins the field,
His naked breast stands for a shield.
His battering shot are babish cries,
His arrows looks of weeping eyes.
His martial ensigns, cold and need;
And feeble flesh his warrior's steed.

His Camp is pitched in a stall,
Be his bulwark but a broken wall;
The crib his trench, hay stalks his stakes,
Of Shepherds he his muster makes.
And thus as sure his foe to wound,
The Angels' trumps alarum sound.

My soul with Christ join thou in fight,
Stick to the tents that he hath pight.
Within his crib is surest ward –
This little Babe will be thy guard.
If thou wilt foil thy foes with joy
Then flit not from this heavenly boy.

14 December

Come to your heaven you heavenly choirs –
Earth hath the heaven of your desires.
Remove your dwelling to your god,
A stall is now his best abode.
Sith men their homage do deny
Come Angels all their fault supply.

His chilling cold doth heat require;
Come Seraphims in lieu of fire.
This little ark no cover hath
Let Cherubs' wings his body swath.
Come Raphael, this babe must eat;
Provide our little Toby meat.

Let Gabriel be now his groom
That first took up his earthly room.
Let Michael stand in his defence
Whom love hath link'd to feeble sense.
Let graces rock when he doth cry,
And Angels sing his lullaby.

With 'New heaven, new war' we are back to a nativity scene, although the familiar picture derived from Luke's Gospel is built up gradually, almost as a by-product of the rather more immediate landscape that Southwell portrays. This landscape is one of vast scope. Think of Luke's 'multitude of the heavenly host' who accompany the angel's visit to the shepherds (Luke 2.13), and there is Southwell's starting point. He calls on the whole host of heavenly beings and draws their attention down, with ours, to focus on the single image of the baby. It is as though we are in an immense theatre, and this child is illumin-ated by a single spotlight on a darkened stage. We know that the rest of the space on the stage is there, but we cannot see it, for we have not yet been shown what it looks like. Revealing what lies in the darkness is a key theme of the poem.

Angels have a central part to play in the story of Jesus' birth, and frequently appear on Christmas cards. Yet they are often rather stylized in their appearance. Images from illuminated manuscripts or Renaissance paintings are often very beautiful, but far removed from us in time. Neither they nor chubby cherubs with rosy cheeks convey much sense of the actual real-ity of angels in everyday experience. What do they look like? How do they make themselves known?

In seeking to emphasize certain aspects of the birth of Jesus, Southwell draws on the biblical witness to the presence of a variety of heavenly beings. Here are dynamic creatures, each of which has been, and continues to be, directly involved in human life. The seraphim are the fiery beings seen by Isaiah in the Temple, who proclaim the holiness of God. One of them brings a burning coal from the altar and on touching Isaiah's mouth, cleanses him and declares him free of guilt and sin (Isaiah 6.1–7). The 'Cherubs' or cherubim are mentioned numerous times in descriptions of the ark of the covenant and in the furnishings of the Temple. A carved cherub was placed at each end of the mercy-seat, and the wings of each creature provided a covering for this most holy place.

Cherubim appear not simply as statues, though, but as living beings – most notably in the visions of Ezekiel, where again they are directly linked to the presence of God. In the apocryphal book of Tobit, Raphael appears unrecognized as an angel, but provides essential guidance and help to Tobias. Apart from a significant role in the more extraordinary events of the story, he ensures that Tobias has food for his journey. At the end, he reveals himself to be 'Raphael, one of the seven angels who stand ready and enter before the glory of the Lord' (Tobit 12.15). Gabriel is a familiar figure as the one who was sent to tell Mary that she would have a son. He is also the angel who was sent by God to tell Zechariah of the birth of John. Less familiar perhaps is his role in the life of Daniel, where he appears as an interpreter of a vision, and as one who brings wisdom, understanding and reassurance to Daniel (Daniel 8.16; 9.21). Michael too features in the book of Daniel. He is described to Daniel by another angelic being as one of the chief princes, and as a great prince, 'the protector of your people' (Daniel 10.13–21; 12.1). He appears to be involved in conflict between nations at a heavenly level, a belief reflected in the book of Revelation (Revelation 12.7) and the letter of Jude (Jude 9). These are powerful beings, as are the numerous other angelic beings – the speaker who addresses Daniel, for example – who, like Raphael, appear in human form and say that they have been sent by God.

However, the angels are not called on by Southwell to display their power with a show of fire or force. He calls them instead to set aside the majesty to which they are accustomed, and bring their gifts to a particular point on earth's stage. In the darkness of human ignorance and neglect, fiery seraphim will bring warmth, and the wings of cherubs provide a covering. Raphael is summoned to find food, Gabriel to look after the child, and Michael to defend him. Yet in this domestication of heavenly power, there is also a sense of tremendous potential. It is not that these beings are 'cut down to size', but that the identity of this newborn baby is revealed by their presence.

In daily life it is very common to become rather bogged down in earthly matters. 'I know that God is there,' we might say to ourselves, 'and when I've just done this, then I'll be able to stop and pray for a moment.' Often, though, we find that we have never actually got to the point when 'this' has been done. Southwell is well aware of the human lack of attention to heavenly things. The point he is making, however, is that rather than encouraging people to stop and look upwards, the 'heavenly choirs' are to come down. If he conveys at the start of his poem the sense that heaven is 'up there' and earth 'down here', it is only so that he can emphasize that heaven has 'relocated'. Don't look up to the lights, but down to the darkened stage. We cannot see all that is going on, but there is certainly more here than meets the eye.

15 December

This little ark no cover hath
Let Cherubs' wings his body swath.

This morning I lost my car keys at the recycling point in a supermarket car park. They were not in any of my pockets, nor had I left them in the ignition. I checked the bags I had just emptied, and for roughly a whole minute of my life the thought grew in my mind that somehow they were now hidden with the card or the plastic *inside* one of the huge steel containers which are carefully designed not to let things out. I saw my careful plans for the day begin to crumble in the face of much more pressing issues: How was I going to get the keys back? How would I get the car home? It was a very long minute, until I found the keys on the floor of the car near the back seat. (How did they end up there?) The pattern of life reasserted itself, and I heaved a sigh of relief. The thought of something being so thoroughly hidden was not a comfortable one.

The difficulty with the season of Advent is that it can seem just like that – its focus is something which is thoroughly hidden, inaccessible and not very comfortable. Perhaps this is why anticipation of Christmas so often takes over. There is something more tangible about Christmas. We know what it is about, even if we do not believe it. Even if we want no part in the religious observance of Christmas, we can still choose to enjoy celebrations and the exchange of gifts. Advent offers nothing of that kind, however; there is far less to get hold of. It is about hope, and hope is by definition about waiting for something that has not yet happened. The focus of this hope has huge implications. It is about nothing less than the place of God in the world we inhabit. Huge, and yet hidden. In the imagery he uses in this poem, Southwell brings to the fore something which is of central importance to the way we think about this divine presence. He refers to the baby as a 'little ark', and calls on the cherubim to swathe his body with their wings. As it stands it is a lovely image, but a quick scout back through the Bible will enrich it further.

Two different Hebrew words are translated as 'ark'. One is the word used of the huge boat-like structure that Noah made. The other is the word that Southwell is focused on here: the wooden box which was the ark of the covenant. Carried with the Israelites through the Sinai desert and into the land of Canaan, lost and regained in war, and finally housed in Jerusalem, this was the central symbol of the presence of God with his people. It was made to contain the two tablets of the law given to Moses at Sinai. It was a visible reminder of the covenant agreement that God had made with his people, an emblem of that essential relationship.

In Exodus 25 we can read the very precise instructions that God gives to Moses about the construction of the ark. Moses is told to make a 'mercy-seat', which is to be put on top of the ark. Then we read, 'You shall make two cherubim of gold; you shall make them of hammered work, at the two ends of the mercy-seat . . . The cherubim shall spread out their wings above, overshadowing the mercy-seat with their wings' (Exodus 25.18, 20a). All of this material is a focus for one thing: 'There I will meet you, and from above the mercy-seat, from between the two cherubim that are on the ark of the covenant, I will deliver to you all my commands for the Israelites' (Exodus 25.22). The mercy-seat on the ark is the place from which God speaks. It was housed in the holiest part of the tabernacle, set apart from the rest by a curtain embroidered with cherubim, who are always associated with the holiness and glory of God. This was the place of atonement, of presence and of revelation. Leviticus 16 describes how Aaron and his successors are to enter this place once a year and carry out the ceremonies of atonement for the sins of the people, so that they 'shall be clean before the LORD' (Leviticus 16.30).

All of this is encompassed in Southwell's description of the baby Jesus as 'this little ark'. The ark is the location of the mercy-seat, the focus of God's presence with his people. It is the place from where he speaks, and the place from where the whole people of God are cleansed. That is no small claim for the poet to make! His call to these powerful heavenly creatures is not simply to remind us of their reality as part of the unseen aspects of the world we live in. By their attendance they reveal something of the true nature of the child they are called on to serve: this child is the 'place' from where God speaks; this child is the means by which we are cleansed.

As things stand, though, we need reminders of the hidden reality of the child. There will be no actual words of help from a baby yet. But there is something more: small though he may be, in this little person is the presence of God. Is Southwell calling only to the heavenly choirs? Or is he also calling to us, asking us to recognize and acknowledge something which is as yet hidden? The picture that he paints here in words conveys the reality of some others, very familiar:

Your will be done, on earth as it is in heaven.

16 December

This little babe so few days old
Is come to rifle Satan's fold.
All hell doth at his presence quake,
Though he himself for cold do shake.
For in this weak unarmed wise,
The gates of hell he will surprise.

I used to think that this was the beginning of Southwell's poem, and I used to think that it was called 'This little babe'. Like many other people, I first got to know these words through getting to know the music of Benjamin Britten. Along with 'New prince, new pompe' and other poems, these words are set to music in *A Ceremony of Carols*. The sense of agitation conveyed by Britten's music echoes the sense of disturbance we find here, not at the beginning but in the middle of the poem, as Southwell reveals a little more of the scene he is describing.

'New heaven, new war' is a poem full of the sound of voices. Southwell has imagined the voices of the angels enjoying the eternal praise of heaven. He has recalled the sound of the seraphim crying 'Holy, holy, holy' in the Temple. He has reminded us of the voice of Gabriel, advising, encouraging and announcing; and with the image of the ark he has encouraged us to hear the voice of God himself. However, he is clear that this is not the whole story. In this verse he casts a shadow. What does he mean when he talks of 'Satan's fold'? Apart from anything else, he wants us to see that there is another voice around on this stage. This voice is Satan's, a voice we hear in the first two chapters of Job.

For all the horror and challenge of the book of Job, a certain artful, teasing quality is evident in the opening chapters. We see Job on earth, rich in every way. Unbeknownst to him, however, in heaven he is the subject of a conversation between the Lord and Satan. I think it only fair to say that the Lord appears to provoke Satan – asking where he has come from, whether he has seen Job, and pointing out the perfections of the man. Rising to the bait, Satan points out all the reasons Job has to honour God; so in response God allows Satan to use the power he has to put this to the test. We see bad things happen to Job's family and possessions, although with no hint of the cause. At the beginning of the second chapter, exactly the same provoking conversation occurs. This time, God allows Job himself to be in Satan's power, with the one constraint that his life must be spared. It is a picture which exactly sums up the nature of Satan – he appears as a heavenly being with access to God, and is what his name means: the accuser. If heaven is a legal court, then Satan is the prosecutor, a divisive character who seeks to undermine God's authority, and to disrupt the relationships God has with humankind.

In the Bible, just as we saw with the concept of hell, so the idea of Satan develops as time goes on. The Greek translation, *diabolos*, gives us the word 'devil' and images of the kind mentioned earlier. However, I like to hang on to the picture given in these opening chapters of Job as it seems to me that this gets right to the heart of what is essential in understanding Satan. The power of accusation to cause division and breakdown is a reality never far from human relationships.

So what is Satan's 'fold'? Sheep have a firm place in Jesus' teaching, being a central part of everyday life. In John 10, when he is teaching about the relationship of shepherd and sheep, Jesus naturally mentions the familiar sheepfold and gate. Imagine yourself as one of those sheep. With the danger of wild animals around, especially at night, you will find that you are glad to be herded into the safety of the fold. This is probably an enclosure made of stone with an entrance gate, so that along with your sheep companions, you can be shut in for increased security. You know very well the sound of your shepherd's voice. When the sky is lighter and your stomach begins to rumble, you will only leave the fold when he opens the gate and calls you to come out.

When Jesus speaks of the sheepfold and of himself as the shepherd, he is developing this very familiar image. It is not only that sheep were central to agricultural life in Palestine at that time, but that the leaders of the Israelites were traditionally referred to as shepherds. God was known as the true shepherd of Israel. The prophet Ezekiel probably offers the fullest exposition of this theme. In chapter 34 the false shepherds of Israel are condemned and are contrasted with God, the true shepherd, whose care for his sheep is emphasized.

Three more points are made. First, there will be judgement between the beasts of the flock; not all will continue to belong to God. Second, God promises to set up his servant David as the shepherd of the people. Third, he promises that he will make 'a covenant of peace' with the sheep of his flock, which will bring freedom, security and blessing. All of these resonate in Jesus' words in John. Like those who heard him then, we are provoked to consider where we stand. Are we among those who respond only to the voice of the true shepherd, or do we pay more attention to the sound of other voices calling?

If we were present before God with the heavenly beings, as Satan is at the beginning of Job, we might be able to see who belongs to which fold. Most of the time, though, things are not so clear cut. We cannot know who belongs where; we do not know enough to make such definite judgements. Too many loud voices are too quick to proclaim who belongs to which fold – Satan's fold or the fold of the Shepherd. One thing is evident though: in asserting that all hell will quake at the presence of this baby, Southwell makes it quite clear that it is not only in the heavenly sphere that the baby's true nature is recognized. For the most part, however, we are in the position of Job, lacking the clear perspective of heaven's gaze. Like Job, are we willing to stand up for what is true against the voices that will seek to accuse and undermine us?

17 December

With tears he fights and wins the field,
His naked breast stands for a shield.
His battering shot are babish cries,
His arrows looks of weeping eyes.
His martial ensigns, cold and need;
And feeble flesh his warrior's steed.

His Camp is pitched in a stall,
Be his bulwark but a broken wall;
The crib his trench, hay stalks his stakes,
Of Shepherds he his muster makes.
And thus as sure his foe to wound,
The Angels' trumps alarum sound.

The scene has changed, and the emphasis moved from heaven to earth. The lights have come fully up, and the stage is set with the trappings of a sixteenth-century battlefield. It is a bit like the battle scene towards the end of the film of *The Lion, the Witch and the Wardrobe* where forces true to Aslan are fighting those on the side of the Witch. As in that scene, here Southwell evokes infantry armed with bows and arrows, and cavalry ready for the charge. Shields glitter in the sunlight, and in the background are pitched the tents of the enemy's camp. Flags are raised, the bugle heralding the onset of battle is about to be heard. But here, in the centre of it all, is the baby.

It is madness of course; a crazy scene. What might Southwell have written now, if like us he was familiar with scenes of battle in Iraq, Afghanistan or Libya?

With tears he fights and wins the field,
His naked breast stands for a bullet-proof vest.
His surface-to-air missiles are babish cries,
His machine-gun fire looks of weeping eyes.
His badges of war, cold and need;
And feeble flesh his armoured tank.

Southwell would have written good poetry, which of course this is not, but it highlights the point. He is showing us war, with a newborn baby right at the heart of it, and the claim that this child is certain to win the battle.

Southwell loves to bring incompatible images together. Of course the focal point of Christmas is a baby, but I have never seen a Christmas card showing a baby in the middle of a sixteenth-century battle. Why would anyone want to do that? Here, though, is a poet who loves to make us question our faith, and to make a particular theological point. Yes, the child fights, but not in the ways we might think. Everything that is said here, Southwell's itemizing of the tools and landscape of war, points us towards something rather different from that suggested by this imagery. The clue to the kind of fight that is meant lies in the phrase 'The Angels' trumps'.

Trumpets are probably not the first things we are likely to think of in the context of war, but their use in proclaiming the onset of an event goes back to biblical times. The story of the battle for Jericho in Joshua 6 is one of the most memorable examples. Apart from the proclamation of war, however, trumpets were very much a part of the worship of the people. In Psalm 81.3 we find the command to blow the trumpet at the festal day. Not surprisingly, perhaps, they also have a very specific role in the imagery of the end-time. When Southwell speaks here of 'The Angels' trumps', he is very much in keeping with the language and imagery that Paul uses when he writes to Christians in Thessalonica.

In 1 Thessalonians 4.16 Paul itemizes three signs of the coming of God: 'For the Lord himself, with a cry of command, with the archangel's call and with the sound of God's trumpet, will descend from heaven, and the dead in Christ will rise first.' Similarly, when writing to Christians in Corinth about the resurrection, he speaks of our transformation as happening 'in a moment, in the twinkling of an eye, at the last trumpet. For the trumpet will sound, and the dead will be raised imperishable, and we will be changed' (1 Corinthians 15.52). Just like today, both Corinth and Thessalonica were places with a variety of religious views jostling for prominence. From the way Paul writes we can see the kinds of questions people there had about faith and how to live it out. In these two passages he is addressing the particular issue of future hope. What difference did the resurrection of Jesus make? If Jesus is coming back to finish in some way what God has begun in him, what about people who have already died? Will they miss out? Paul is of course a Jew, immersed in the teachings of his faith. He repeats the Jewish conviction of the end-time activity of God, found, for example, in Joel 2.1–2, Zephaniah 1.14–16 and Zechariah 9.14. The apocalyptic language and imagery – trumpets included – convey a firm conviction that God will act to deal with idolatry and injustice, and set his creation right.

Here, in his use of the trumpet imagery, Southwell ties two ideas together: the idea of the decisive end-time battle, and the Incarnation. It is the baby, only a few days old, who comes to plunder the fold of Satan and who sets hell quaking. Southwell takes the powerful imagery of the battlefield and harnesses it to something which is most vulnerable. We began by highlighting the battle imagery in these verses, but if we take the other half of each statement, we have tears, an unprotected naked breast, babish cries, weeping eyes, cold, need and feeble flesh. The battle setting for this baby is a stall with a broken wall, a crib with stalks of hay, and the only adults mentioned are the shepherds. This is hardly what we expect of warriors ready for war, and perhaps that is just the point. In presenting it this way, Southwell challenges our expectations. He challenges what we believe about heavenly beings, he challenges our belief about angels and Satan, and above all he challenges our ideas about power. We are firmly back in the traditional nativity scene, in the fold of the true shepherd.

18 December

My soul with Christ join thou in fight,
Stick to the tents that he hath pight.
Within his crib is surest ward –
This little Babe will be thy guard.
If thou wilt foil thy foes with joy
Then flit not from this heavenly boy.

When John describes the meeting between Jesus and his first two disciples, he includes an invitation and a response. When they follow him to see where he is staying, Jesus invites them to 'come and see'. John tells us that they came, they saw, and they remained with him (John 1.35–39). This is not just about basic hospitality. The themes of coming to Jesus, seeing things for what they really are and remaining with him are central to John's understanding of Jesus' life. Later in the Gospel, Jesus uses the imagery of the vine to reiterate this intimate relationship (chapter 15). If the disciples remain in him, then like the branch which is part of the vine, they will be abundantly fruitful.

This same invitation has a resonance in the final verse of 'New heaven, new war', where Southwell exhorts himself to join the battle with Christ that he has illustrated in the previous two verses; 'join thou', 'stick to' and 'flit not' are all commands to remain firm – not only in intention but in action too. Whereas at the opening of the poem he addressed the vast company of heaven, here in the more confined space of the earthly cattle stall, he addresses a single entity, his own soul. The implications of involvement are clear. His illustration of the vast scale of these divine actions nevertheless has its focus in a single human life. He may not address his hearers directly, but he makes it quite clear that there is no reason for anyone to claim that the scale of events is just too large for us to cope with. God has chosen to act in the life of Jesus, and through Jesus we are all, like those first disciples, invited to join in.

Is this not rather scary though? There are no trappings of security here. In addressing his soul, Southwell urges us not to look around for other places to pitch a tent. We are not to side with anyone or anything else. There may be other places and things which are more congenial, but he wants us to stay with the tents pitched by Christ, not to find an alternative. More specifically still, he claims that the safest place to be is in the crib, where 'this little Babe' will guard us. Typically, he exploits the paradox of the Incarnation. He has already made it quite clear that the Babe is just that – a baby, as dependent on others for basic needs as any other baby. Yet here, in the place of greatest vulnerability, is the place of greatest safety. Stay with him, commands Southwell.

The importance of remaining in Christ is evident in Paul's writing too. He travelled widely in Asia Minor and the Near East and, as we have already said, much of his letter writing was taken up with addressing particular concerns of Christian faith and practice. People had become Christians from a mix of pagan and Jewish backgrounds and needed advice on how to live in their new-found faith. We quite often find Paul urging them to put former practices behind them. Some things were incompatible with their new life in Christ. More than once he uses the image of clothing to illustrate this. Paul reminds the church in Ephesus, 'You were taught to put away your former way of life . . . and to clothe yourselves with the new self, created according to the likeness of God in true righteousness and holiness' (Ephesians 4.22–24). Again, writing to the church in Colossae, he says, 'As God's chosen ones, holy and beloved, clothe yourselves with compassion, kindness, humility, meekness, and patience' (Colossians 3.12). These are the 'clothes' that help to mark us out as people who are sticking to Christ, people who in Paul's language are 'in Christ'.

But it is not just clothing that God provides for people who identify themselves with 'this little Babe' who is in the crib. Southwell encourages us to join in the fight, and God gives the armour that we need for that fight. Again in Ephesians, Paul urges people to put on the whole armour of God. He mentions particularly the belt of truth to go round the waist, and the breastplate of righteousness. He urges us to take the shield of faith, the helmet of salvation and the sword of the Spirit (Ephesians 6.13–17). Paul uses very similar images in writing to the church in Thessalonica (1 Thessalonians 5.8). This battle to which Southwell calls us is to be fought with righteousness, truth, faith, love and hope of salvation. Above all, at its heart is the proclamation of the gospel of peace.

We are never far from the paradox at the heart of our faith. No one wins a battle by keeping still. When Southwell calls us to join in the fight, it is not one that will be won by trying to *hide* in the crib. It is about being there in order to be equipped for action. This fight, though, should not generate fear. It is something that we are to embark on with joy. While the end of his first letter to the Thessalonians may be full of warnings and exhortations to be ready, awake and armed, Paul goes on to urge his hearers to rejoice: 'Rejoice always, pray without ceasing, give thanks in all circumstances; for this is the will of God in Christ Jesus for you' (1 Thessalonians 5.16–18).

We end where we began, with angels. Those disciples mentioned earlier went and found their friends, and some of them went to Jesus too. It is clear that while they recognize something special in him, he also recognizes something in them – something of the true self. At the end of John chapter 1, Jesus makes a promise to Nathanael: 'Very truly, I tell you, you will see heaven opened and the angels of God ascending and descending upon the Son of Man.' Neither the first disciples nor John's first hearers would have missed the allusion to Jacob's dream, described in Genesis 28. In the dream Jacob sees a ladder going between earth and heaven on which the angels of God are going up and down. When he awakes, he names the place Bethel, which means 'house of God'. As Southwell draws his poem to a close, I have no doubt that with the spotlight on the baby he is declaring like Jacob, 'This is none other than the house of God, and this is the gate of heaven.'

'Hills of the north, rejoice!' by Charles Edward Oakley (1832–65)

Hills of the north, rejoice,
echoing songs arise,
hail with united voice
him who made earth and skies:
he comes in righteousness and love,
he brings salvation from above.

Isles of the southern seas
sing to the listening earth,
carry on every breeze
hope of a world's new birth:
in Christ shall all be made anew,
his word is sure,
his promise true.

Lands of the east, arise,
he is your brightest morn,
greet him with joyous eyes,
praise shall his path adorn:
the God whom you have longed to know
in Christ draws near, and calls you now.

Shores of the utmost west,
lands of the setting sun,
welcome the heavenly guest
in whom the dawn has come:
he brings a never-ending light
who triumphed o'er our darkest night.

Shout, as you journey on,
songs be in every mouth,
lo, from the north they come,

from east and west and south:
in Jesus all shall find their rest,
in him the longing earth be blest.

(adapted)

19 December

Hills of the north, rejoice,
echoing songs arise,
hail with united voice
him who made earth and skies:
he comes in righteousness and love,
he brings salvation from above.

This hymn brings a blast of fresh air into the all too pervasive anticipation of Christmas. With its unflinching conviction of the strength of the presence of God, it has the same feel as the passage from Isaiah 35. If Advent focuses on the fact that something is going to happen, then the words of this hymn help us to explore what that might be. In its majestic imagery we are given a vision of the whole created order being involved in this happening. In its focus on the natural world, we are encouraged to consider how human beings might also respond.

I was recently involved in a drama workshop based on the narrative of Jesus' death in Mark's Gospel. We were talking about the crowds in Jerusalem, those who welcomed Jesus and those who later in the week called for the release of Barabbas. We asked ourselves why they were there, and what they might have been thinking. In a world of broadband and mobile phones, MP3 players, YouTube, Facebook and Twitter, it is hard to imagine having to leave your house to get news of what is going on in the world. Yet that is how it was. You went out and asked a neighbour, or else you saw a crowd gathering and went to find out what was going on. You got caught up in the momentum of the whole group, and were carried along by being physically present as whatever it was took place.

This is how I feel when I read the words of this hymn. Whatever it is that is happening involves the whole world. I am caught up in its movement. The vision is vast, taking us to each point of the compass in turn, and only at the end do we have the whole picture. Only at the end do we stop moving, and come to rest. So what event is going on here? Someone is coming, and that someone is none other than the Creator. He is characterized by righteousness and love, and with him he brings salvation. This thing that is happening is nothing less than the second coming.

I expect that I should say, 'Wow!' but I have to confess to a niggling unease about the whole idea of 'the second coming'. What does it mean now? Exploring the answer to that question will take more than just today's reflection, and we will come to it again tomorrow. Let us start by thinking about what it means to proclaim that we will greet 'him who made earth and skies'. This phrase may conjure up images of Genesis 1 and 2, and the beauty of the natural world. Yet what about urban life, where we may see more tarmac and tall buildings than 'earth and skies'? To speak of God as the creative force within the whole created world must be equally relevant to the spheres of commerce and education, hospitals and finance, fossil fuel extraction and industry, manufacturing and advanced technologies. This is the world of aircraft, shipping, road and rail traffic; of the business of government and entertainment; of famine, warfare and natural disaster. Any claims we make about the nature of God and of our faith have to be true in the reality of all of this, and our religious practice must not be kept isolated from it.

The belief in the second coming which we explore through this hymn is deeply rooted in the reality of human experience, good and bad. It is a belief that has been around for a very long time. The voice of the prophet in the later chapters of Isaiah offers insights which are as relevant today as they were two and a half thousand years ago. Over time, God's people had experienced political and social uncertainty and challenge: loss of political independence, invasion by foreign empires and, for some, exile. Others had never left but had witnessed the destruction of their Temple and its worship. The last eleven chapters of Isaiah bear witness to those trying to remain faithful to God and struggling with the very mixed environment in which they were living. Some of these passages are strikingly up to date in terms of the kind of challenges that might face us in daily life now. In addressing those living in the province of Judaea, the prophet is clear that some people were engaged in deceitfulness, in idolatry, in acts of violence and in the perversion of the judicial system. Isaiah 59.3–8 offers a cutting analysis of the situation, followed by a wonderfully vivid lament.

> We grope like the blind along a wall . . .
> Justice is turned back, and righteousness stands at a
>   distance;
> for truth stumbles in the public square.
>
> (Isaiah 59.10, 14)

There is disillusion about the morality of public life, and a sense of everyone going about in the dark. The prophet is quite clear about the reason for this lack of clarity and direction. It is not that God is not willing, but that the people have turned from him, putting up such barriers by their behaviour that they can no longer see nor hear him (Isaiah 59.2, 12–13). In this challenging situation it is not surprising that those striving to be faithful reach back into the past in order to reaffirm not just the power of God but the love of God for his people. 'Hills of the north, rejoice' celebrates the creative power of God, but this belief is not simply about the origins of things. This is the characteristic that was seen in the action of God in the Exodus – the power to redeem, to save and to create a new relationship. For the prophet in Isaiah there is not a flicker of doubt that God is present and will act, just as he was present and acted in the past.

It may seem that we have strayed rather far from the idea of the second coming as expressed in this hymn, but this does answer one of my 'niggles'. If the second coming is not simply wishful thinking, then it is of fundamental importance that it be anchored in what we already know of God. This means looking back before we look forward, and seeing whether there is consistency in the claims people have made in the past about God. The righteousness and love which the hymn writer mentions are seen by the prophet too. Certainly the prophet talks of vengeance, but it stems from God's anger at the injustices he sees in this rather messy human community. There is no suggestion that this is about anything other than the consequences of the conduct already mentioned. As we have seen elsewhere, anger and love are frequently intertwined. All of this is part of the salvation that God will bring:

> And he will come to Zion as Redeemer,
> to those in Jacob who turn from transgression.
>
> (Isaiah 59.20)

If there is any question mark at all, it is over who will let him in.

20 December

Isles of the southern seas
sing to the listening earth,
carry on every breeze
hope of a world's new birth:
in Christ shall all be made anew,
his word is sure, his promise true.

Lands of the east, arise,
he is your brightest morn,
greet him with joyous eyes,
praise shall his path adorn:
the God whom you have longed to know
in Christ draws near, and calls you now.

These verses are full of joy and hope. They chime in with that spine-tingling feeling I mentioned in the Preface, but rather than evoking a night sky, here it is more like a morning in late winter when we can smell the promise of spring in the air. The air carries within it a scent of new growth, and the heart lifts, reassured by the knowledge that spring will come. The imagery works equally well for those who live near to the equator or who, in the southern hemisphere, live out Advent in the heat of summer. Where that heat is stultifying, the freshness of the months that follow can carry that same welcome sense of change and newness. Before it arrives, though, there is often a moment which can catch us unawares. It is the hint of something about to happen. It requires us to stop, to listen, and to engage all our senses as we try to become attuned to what this might be.

I remember as a child of about ten making some complaint to my mum about a friendship. She suggested that I telephone the friend concerned to sort it out. When I rejected this sensible suggestion, naturally she asked why. While I have no memory of the particular problem, I clearly remember the reason I gave for not phoning: it was because I could not see the other person. It was true, although it felt like an admission of weakness. Years on, I have come to realize that the great differences of personality and temperament between people affect even such mundane things as making phone calls. I know that I much prefer talking face to face, because there is so much about communication which is not simply about hearing a voice. The expression on a person's face when speaking, gestures and body language, the physical surroundings – all add such a lot to the spoken words. I like to see as well as hear. These verses of 'Hills of the north' suggest to me the same kind of attentive activity: the same kind of 'edge of the seat' watching and waiting, the same eagerness to find out what is going on. It is as if the earth is one step ahead: listening and responding to something which we are slow to understand.

One of the convictions expressed in the hymn is that of new creation: the world shall be made new in Christ. Paul talks a lot in his letters about being 'in Christ'. This phrase encapsulates everything about how different life is when it is lived from the perspective of being a disciple of Jesus. Paul also talks about the created world itself. In a familiar passage in Romans 8, he speaks of the creation having been 'subjected to futility' by God (verse 20). To state the obvious, everything in the created world is subject to change and decay. We die; trees and plants die; green places become desert; machines wear out and have to be replaced, and so on. Yet Paul goes on to speak of the hope 'that the creation itself will be set free from its bondage to decay and will obtain the freedom of the glory of the children of

God' (verse 21). Paul has already made it clear that this hope is rooted in the resurrection of Jesus (in Romans 6.8–10, for example) – which is not simply a one-off, but a pledge of the possibility for all human life.

Whether we talk in theological terms, as I have been doing here, or speak of quantum theory and laws governing the behaviour and relationships between sub-atomic particles, we are looking on to the same landscape, albeit through different windows. That landscape is the Advent landscape. To be there is to inhabit one kind of life with the awareness that there is also more to come: a fullness of life given by God and demonstrated in the resurrection of Jesus. I am not going to try to tackle here questions of how science and faith relate to one another – it is too huge a subject and my scientific knowledge is too weak. Suffice it to say that I welcome the revelations of scientific pursuit, and see no conflict between science and theology.

My childhood dislike of the telephone was matched by a love of receiving letters. I still treasure letters I received as a child from a friend who moved away when I was seven. Nearly two thousand years on we still have some of Paul's letters, written to various church communities, mostly in the eastern Mediterranean. We can read them in the New Testament and hear his passion, his longings and his frustrations. He could not always be physically present, but he was very much in touch. He had a relationship with the communities and individual people he wrote to, and cared deeply about what happened to them. This Advent hymn emphasizes the importance of relationship in the concept of the second coming. The second coming is not an optional extra to Christian faith, but an essential part of it. God's relationship with the universe is rooted in his creativity, as is his desire to bring about new birth.

> The God whom you have longed to know
> in Christ draws near, and calls you now.

This is about divine initiative, not simply about human dreams. When Jesus spoke of himself and his ministry in the synagogue in Nazareth (Luke 4), he was quoting Isaiah 61:

> The spirit of the Lord GOD is upon me,
> because the LORD has anointed me;
> he has sent me to bring good news to the oppressed,
> to bind up the broken-hearted,
> to proclaim liberty to the captives,
> and release to the prisoners.   (Isaiah 61.1)

It is as if the longings of broken humanity and divine love are two sides of a coin. Crucifixion and resurrection are what happen when these two come together.

21 December

Shores of the utmost west,
lands of the setting sun,
welcome the heavenly guest
in whom the dawn has come:
he brings a never-ending light
who triumphed o'er our darkest night.

We have now spent three weeks living the season of Advent, yet even though we are so close to Christmas itself, the imagery in this verse of the Advent hymn points not to the nativity but to the resurrection. The images of light in Isaiah 60 are certainly present in the background, but it is Luke's two disciples on the road to Emmaus who are most evident here (Luke 24.13–35).

It was the time of Passover, a major religious festival. Lots of Jews came from the countryside into Jerusalem to celebrate one of the foundations of their faith: the power of God to save his people, based on the experience many years before when, through Moses, God led them out of Egypt and forged a new relationship with them as they travelled in the Sinai desert. By now, this relationship, sealed by the covenant, had identified them for hundreds of years. Passover was therefore a dangerous time – at least from the point of view of the Roman overlords in Judaea. Considerable numbers of extra people in the city, all celebrating freedom from oppression delivered by the hand of God, meant that the potential for trouble was high. The slightest hint of agitation needed careful handling lest it develop into full-scale rebellion. Hints of trouble there had been, and a murky mixture of motives in various quarters. The result: the arrest of Jesus by night, the release of the rebel fighter Barabbas to placate the crowd, and the crucifixion of Jesus after a trial behind closed doors.

Imagine yourself as one of these two. The stranger you meet on the road appears to be ignorant of the arrest and death of Jesus. You stop in your tracks. Can he really know nothing about it? To you it seems that in just a few days everything has gone from good to the worst state imaginable. The things you heard and witnessed and were involved in with Jesus had given you such hope for the future, and yet you have watched them unravelling before your very eyes, ending in the absolute finality of death. You and your friends were still in shock when the women came that morning with talk of an empty tomb and angelic messengers. You have no idea what to do with such a claim. No wonder you and your companion are heading out of the city – perhaps going home.

I wonder how long the seven-mile walk to Emmaus seemed that afternoon, and how Cleopas and his companion felt when the stranger talked them through their scriptures, interpreting and explaining as they walked. I am not sure that I would have had the emotional strength to cope with the roller-coaster of hope and despair that those last few days had brought. Yet if what he was saying was true, then they could not simply let him go. The explanation seemed to back up the claims of the women, yet it was all too new, too much to take in quickly, too much to hope for, perhaps. As it was about sunset when they arrived at their destination, they offered a welcome, which he accepted.

When he was at the table with them, he took bread, blessed and broke it, and gave it to them. Then their eyes were opened, and they recognized him; and he vanished from their sight. They said to each other, 'Were not our hearts burning within us while he was talking to us on the road, while he was opening the scriptures to us?'

(Luke 24.30–32)

Inside the house, things changed. There is something necessarily intellectual about interpreting the scriptures; even those of us who do not think of it in this way use our intellect in the process of reading, and some of us positively enjoy intellectual activity. Perhaps, had the circumstances been a little different, I might have suggested to the stranger that we nip back to Jerusalem, find a few friendly rabbis in the Temple courts and get out the scrolls containing the commentaries – then we could have a *proper* debate about all of this. Who would say no to a bit of quality time with Jesus *and* the collected insights of those who have spent long hours studying and debating the diverse texts of the Bible? The trouble is, it was not like that, and Luke's telling makes clear the limits of intellectual understanding alone. These two do not know what to think. Yet in accepting their invitation of hospitality, and in the blessing and breaking of bread, Jesus is seen for who he truly is. Revelation and recognition come together, and their whole outlook is transformed. They understand something of which earlier they had only dimly been aware. Now, they recognize the feeling of their hearts burning within as he talked – a counterpart to the stranger's exasperated criticism of their being 'slow of heart'.

There have been plenty of times when I have been at church managing young children in the pew, or in the 'toy room' at the back (where sound comes in by way of a speaker, but not out – well, mostly not). In those circumstances I have often wondered why I bother to be there, but the answer is always the same. It is because in that moment when I hold out my hands to receive the gift of God in bread and wine, I know that being there is better than not. I have sometimes not been able to say anything more than that and it has felt like holding on by a thread, but it has always taken me back to something fundamental about Christian faith. God is compassionate, and God has taken the initiative. It may be that we can do no more than open a tiny crack in the door, yet that may be just enough to welcome this heavenly guest – and as the hymn reminds us, that is enough to bring about a completely new way of looking at things. Seven miles of walking or not, Cleopas and his companion went right back to the city, their understanding transformed and, no doubt, their hearts still burning.

22 December

Shout, as you journey on,
Songs be in every mouth,
Lo, from the north they come,
From east and west and south:
In Jesus all shall find their rest,
In him the longing earth is blest.

I had a liturgy tutor at college who, rather than speak of a person having died, liked to say that that person had been 'gathered'. It seemed to me that while this was always done with both a gentle and humorous poke in the direction of religiosity, at the same time it reflected a simple and profound belief in what he was saying. Death is not simply about the cessation of life, and loss for those who remain. To speak of people being 'gathered' is to point us towards a picture of the future which is clearly evident in this hymn, and again takes us to the words of Isaiah.

A whole collection of ideas and images clusters around the future hope expressed by the voice of the prophet Isaiah. These include: people being gathered together or streaming to a focal point (2.2–3; 60.3–4); the mountain of the Lord, also called Zion and Jerusalem (2.2–3; all of chapter 60); the glory of the Lord (40.5); the idea of God's people as a light through whom God's salvation reaches to 'the ends of the earth' (49.6); and the creation of a new heaven and earth (65.17). The central idea is that God is at the heart of his new creation, where there will be no more suffering, and that through his people other nations will be drawn to his presence.

The prophet conveys a beautiful picture, yet what are we to make of it? In one of his visions, Ezekiel had watched the glory of God departing from the Temple in Jerusalem. This was an indication that it was no longer considered a fit place for God's presence (Ezekiel 10, especially verses 18–19). This seems to fit in with the disillusionment about public life expressed in Isaiah 59, which we considered with the first verse of this hymn. Yet in the web of Isaiah's ideas, the revealing of the glory of God appears to be central, and we find passages such as this, where Jerusalem is addressed directly:

> Arise, shine; for your light has come,
> and the glory of the LORD has risen upon you.
> For darkness shall cover the earth,
> and thick darkness the peoples;
> but the LORD will arise upon you,
> and his glory will appear over you.
> Nations shall come to your light,
> and kings to the brightness of your dawn.
>
> (Isaiah 60.1–3)

There is always the danger of treating such a picture in the way we all too easily treat a precious work of art. We can go to an art gallery and admire a painting; we can stand before it and allow it to challenge our perceptions. Once outside, however, it is hard to hang on to what we have just seen. Imagine coming out of the National Gallery and down the steps into Trafalgar Square. The noise and hubbub, the conflicting demands on our attention, and exposure to whatever the weather is at the time immediately begin to wear away at the impact of what we experienced inside. It is the same here. We might find that we can admire this picture of the future, but feel that it has little bearing on the reality of everyday life.

The hymn challenges us to think differently. We have already noted that the ideas of salvation and second coming were rooted in the experience of being the people of God. They had their basis in the events of Exodus and covenant. John takes this one step further. In the opening words of his Gospel, he alludes to the giving of the covenant at Sinai when the glory of God settled on the mountain (Exodus 34). There, the people are instructed to remain below, and there is a sense that the cloud in which the Lord appears protects Moses from the fullness of God's presence. John draws a contrast between Jesus and Moses, pointing out that it is Jesus who is now the focal point of the presence of God with his people:

> And the Word became flesh and lived among us, and we have seen his glory, the glory as of a father's only son, full of grace and truth ... The law indeed was given through Moses; grace and truth came through Jesus Christ.
>
> (John 1.14, 17)

In narrating Jesus' ministry, however, John is clear that the revelation of this glory is only partial. Four times in the first part of the Gospel we are told that Jesus' hour has not yet come. There is a change, however, following the resurrection of Lazarus. Four times after that Jesus speaks of the hour having come. The first of these is in public, to some Greeks who had come to Jerusalem for the Passover festival. 'The hour has come for the Son of Man to be glorified', says Jesus, and he speaks of how a seed needs to die in the earth in order to bear fruit (John 12.23–24). There are two more references to 'the hour' in his teaching to the disciples, and then, finally, before John narrates Jesus' betrayal and arrest, he writes that Jesus prays, 'Father, the hour has come; glorify your Son so that the Son may glorify you, since you have given him authority over all people, to give eternal life to all whom you have given him'

(John 17.1–2). It is quite clear that the moment of glory is also the moment of death, *because* it is only through his death that new life can come.

Finally to Paul: he spends quite a bit of time in his first letter to the church in Corinth reiterating the absolute centrality of the resurrection of Jesus. In chapter 15 he talks about people's experiences of the resurrection, he traces the logic of it, he addresses pastoral concerns, and uses the imagery of the seed, as Jesus did. In all of this Paul speaks theologically: this demonstration of new creation is at the heart of God's nature and activity. Paul wants to make it quite clear that the resurrection of Jesus is the point from which all of this other newness will flow: 'for as all die in Adam, so all will be made alive in Christ. But each in his own order: Christ the first fruits, then at his coming those who belong to Christ' (1 Corinthians 15.22–23). We are back to the image of gathering: just as the farmer gathers his harvest, so God will gather the fruit of his creativity.

It would be easy to go on, but the end of the hymn calls us to rest. Its final words echo Paul's:

> In Jesus all shall find their rest,
> in him the longing earth be blest.

'Child of the stable's secret birth' by Timothy Dudley-Smith (b. 1926)

Child of the stable's secret birth,
the Lord by right of the lords of earth,
let angels sing of a King new-born –
the world is weaving a crown of thorn:
a crown of thorn for that infant head
cradled soft in the manger bed.

Eyes that shine in the lantern's ray;
a face so small in its nest of hay –
face of a child, who is born to scan
the world of men through the eyes of man:
and from that face in the final day
earth and heaven shall flee away.

Voice that rang through the courts on high
contracted now to a wordless cry;
a voice to master the wind and wave,
the human heart and the hungry grave:
the voice of God through the cedar trees
rolling forth as the sound of seas.

Child of the stable's secret birth,
the Father's gift to a wayward earth,
to drain the cup in a few short years
of all our sorrows, our sins and tears –
ours the prize for the road he trod:
ris'n with Christ; at peace with God.

23 December

Child of the stable's secret birth,
the Lord by right of the lords of earth,
let angels sing of a King new-born –
the world is weaving a crown of thorn:
a crown of thorn for that infant head
cradled soft in the manger bed.

Voice that rang through the courts on high
contracted now to a wordless cry;
a voice to master the wind and wave,
the human heart and the hungry grave:
the voice of God through the cedar trees
rolling forth as the sound of seas.

Secrets are funny things. They can be terribly exciting or a huge burden. They might be temporary or might be permanent. The consequences of revealing a secret might lead to great joy or be very harmful. The importance of confession in a religious context is often about providing a safe and confidential place in which secrets can be told, often to the great relief of the teller.

This time of year will be one of positive secrecy for many people. Gifts are hidden away, the delight of opening wrapped parcels is contemplated, and with only two days to go the wait can begin to seem almost unbearable – especially where young children are concerned. In this hymn, we return to the nativity scene in the stable. Just as Southwell urged us to look carefully and see beyond the outward appearance of the characters, so here we are to consider the secret that the stable holds.

Again we need to ask ourselves a question: What is it that we see when we look at the baby lying in a trough for cattle feed, and when we look at his parents and attendants? The first secret that the stable holds is told by the angels, who herald his birth as they would God himself. This baby is Lord and King – although, as we have already noted, there is nothing in the setting that suggests even a hint of that. The second secret that the stable holds is to do with the nature of that kingship. One of the reasons why these verses by Timothy Dudley-Smith are so powerful is that they are full of pregnant phrases which convey so much more than we see in the stable scene itself: 'the world is weaving a crown of thorn' is one such phrase.

In their passion narratives, each of the four Gospels describes Jesus being dressed up and mocked. Matthew, Mark and John specifically mention a crown of thorns being placed on his head by the soldiers. In John's account of the Passion, the kingship of Jesus is a particularly prominent theme. Five times in the course of Pilate's interrogation Jesus is referred to as the King of the Jews. This includes two responses by Jesus on the nature of kingship and power. When Jesus is crucified, Pilate has a sign put up on the cross reading, 'Jesus of Nazareth, the King of the Jews'. John points out that some among the Jewish authorities want this notice altered to read, 'This man said, I am King of the Jews', reducing it from a statement of identity to a matter of personal opinion. This brief scene illuminates that pregnant phrase, 'the world is weaving a crown of thorn', by placing side by side the two perspectives on Jesus which have continued to challenge believers from that day to this.

There have always been plenty of people for whom Jesus has no significance, and for whom his claims of kingship are a matter for mockery. There have always been others who wholeheartedly accept Jesus as King, yet even here we have to be careful to listen to what he himself has said about the nature of this kingship. When asked by Pilate what he has done, Jesus answers, 'My kingdom is not from this world. If my kingdom were from this world, my followers would be fighting to keep me from being handed over to the Jews. But as it is, my kingdom is not from here' (John 18.36). In a further round of questions, Pilate asserts his power to release or to crucify Jesus but, again, Jesus challenges Pilate's understanding of power: 'You would have no power over me unless it had been given you from above' (John 19.11).

Jesus' words to Pilate redefine the nature of kingship and power along lines which are unnatural in a world where the verbal assertion of authority is so often reinforced by a show of force. The crown of thorns remains a potent symbol of the pain of mockery for those who persist in standing up for what is true. For some, their refusal to deny Jesus' kingship will lead to death. For most of us, it presents a day to day challenge which will never lead to physical pain but may cause other difficulties. As Southwell did in other ways, these words provoke us to consider again where the lines of authority lie in our lives. The kingship and power which Jesus speaks of are rooted in the life of God, not in the arena of human conduct. These are not always compatible. Where do we draw the line which we will not cross over? To what extent are we part of the world which goes on weaving a crown of thorns?

Yet if contemplating the kingship of Jesus has taken a rather sombre turn, we are soon reminded of that life of God in which it is rooted. In the 'Voice that rang through the courts on high' we hear God's splendid rant at Job out of the whirlwind (Job 38, 39). We hear echoes of Psalm 29 where the voice of God is mentioned seven times and the kingship and majesty of God are asserted. We hear Jesus' command to the storm (Matthew 8.23–27), and the voice that responds to human need and calls Lazarus from the grave (John 11). Each of these reaches back to the creation itself, where it is the voice of God which calls all things into being.

I suspect that it may not have been much of a secret that a young woman who had been looking for a place to stay had given birth in a stable – nor of much interest either. The secret is not the birth itself, but the identity of the baby.

24 December: Christmas Eve

Eyes that shine in the lantern's ray;
a face so small in its nest of hay –
face of a child, who is born to scan
the world of men through the eyes of man:
and from that face in the final day
earth and heaven shall flee away.

Behind the high altar in Coventry Cathedral hangs a tapestry by Graham Sutherland. At nearly 23 metres high and just over 11.5 metres wide it is huge, and fills the back wall. It depicts Christ in glory, around whose throne are the four living creatures described in Revelation 4. The face of Christ is striking, suggesting kindness, strength, security and serenity. The picture is ambiguous. Christ is enthroned in glory, yet is he seated, standing or lying? Around the vast figure of Christ is a band of gold. No one could doubt that he is very much alive, and yet the shape of this band of gold has always reminded me of a coffin. Christ himself is clothed in white garments, yet they are not the conventional long, flowing robes of a king. Are these the white garments of heaven mentioned in the vision in Revelation, or are they the linen cloths in which the body of Jesus was wrapped prior to burial? Perhaps it was because my visits as a child often came at Christmas, but it always seemed to me that they were like swaddling bands, and the 'coffin' shape encompassing Jesus was the shape of a manger.

This tapestry does something that is also evident in this verse of the hymn: in a single image, vast themes lie together. Without taking our eyes off the manger, we move from the intimacy of a baby's birth to the transformation of the whole created order. Just as, in the cathedral, it seems that the eyes of the enthroned Jesus see you wherever you are, so the eyes of the baby will see across the whole scope of this 'world of men'. We have thought quite a lot through Advent about what we see when we look at the nativity scene, but I wonder what those eyes see when they look out at us.

One way biblical writers explore that question is by speaking of the face of God. To speak of the face of a person is to indicate the nature of the relationship, and 'looking upon' is a mark of bestowing favour. When speaking of God this is often expressed in terms of light. In Psalm 80, in the plea that God will restore his people, three times we hear: 'let your face shine, that we may be saved' (verses 3, 7, 19). The words of the blessing God gives for Aaron contain the prayer that 'the LORD make his face to shine upon you . . . the LORD lift up his countenance upon you' (Numbers 6.25–26). In contrast, Leviticus 20 records the promise that the Lord will set his face against the people if various idolatrous practices are carried out. The relationship will be disrupted because things that are incompatible with the holiness of God have got in the way.

It is in describing the relationship with Moses, however, that the significance of the face is illustrated. We have already been reminded of Moses' surprise and reluctance to do what God asked of him. Yet if it was no easy task getting the Israelites away from Pharaoh and out of Egypt, it was no easier leading them through the Sinai desert. Notwithstanding the signs of God's presence with them, their complaints eventually took the form of demanding a god they could see. The result was the golden calf, and the anger of Moses and God. Their relationship differed from all others. When inside the tent of meeting, 'the LORD used to speak to Moses face to face, as one speaks to a friend' (Exodus 33.11). When returning from Mount Sinai with the tablets the second time, 'the skin of his face shone because he had been talking with God'. Such was the brilliance of his face that he had to wear a veil to protect the people (Exodus 34.29–35).

The New Testament writers pick up this theme of the sometimes hidden reality of the light of God. For them, as for Dudley-Smith, this light is seen in Jesus. The light in the eyes of the baby in its 'nest of hay' may be tiny, but it shines in a way that the lantern will never do. These words are a reflection on the fact that the light, although mostly hidden during Jesus' lifetime, testifies to an existence which encompasses the whole of the human arena, rather than being encompassed by it as we might expect. Occasionally this is glimpsed by Jesus' closest companions. In describing Jesus' appearance with Moses and Elijah, Matthew tells us that 'his face shone like the sun' (Matthew 17.2). Luke says that 'the appearance of his face changed' and those with Jesus 'saw his glory' (Luke 9.29, 32). This light, though, is more than the reflection of divine glory borne by Moses. It is the light of creation itself, the light which, as John says, shines in the darkness and has not been overcome.

Paul takes us one step further. We too are offered the possibility of transformation as we stand before the gaze of Jesus. Paul points out how different our situation is from that of the Israelites under Moses. Our experience of the glory of God comes to us through Christ, such that 'all of us, with unveiled faces, seeing the glory of the Lord as though reflected in a mirror, are being transformed into the same image from one degree of glory to another' (2 Corinthians 3.18).

At the start of December we suggested that the sense of something happening is like 'the full blaze of the midday sun'. In the vision he recounts at the beginning of Revelation, John sees 'one like the Son of Man, clothed with a long robe . . . and his face was like the sun shining with full force' (Revelation 1.13–16). We are back to the tapestry with its depiction of birth, burial and resurrection; and from there to the stable. Whatever that 'face so small in its nest of hay' has seen and continues to see, it is clear that there is no room for secrets in this world of divine encounter.

25 December: Christmas Day

Child of the stable's secret birth,
the Father's gift to a wayward earth,
to drain the cup in a few short years
of all our sorrows, our sins and tears –
ours the prize for the road he trod:
ris'n with Christ; at peace with God.

Two days ago the image of the crown of thorns led us to consider the kingship of Jesus. Here again we see how in this king, heralded by angels, conventional ideas of kingship and divinity are undercut. Two images stand out: 'the cup' and the 'wayward earth'.

In just 17 words, Dudley-Smith sums up the ministry of Jesus, and he does so by using the rich imagery of 'the cup'. We need to do a quick hop backwards through the pages of the Bible to understand its resonances. Here is an allusion to Jesus' prayer in Gethsemane, recorded in the first three Gospels. Jesus prays that 'this cup' will either be taken or may pass from him. In John, the arrest of Jesus is followed by a command to put swords away and the words, 'Am I not to drink the cup that the Father has given me?' (John 18.11). Prior to this moment, Jesus used the image only once. Both Matthew and Mark record the request that James and John will be able to sit on either side of Jesus in his glory (Matthew 20.22–23; Mark 10.38–39). In both Gospels, Jesus asks whether they will be able to 'drink the cup' that he will drink. The imagery would not have been lost on them or any Jewish readers of the Gospels. In the Hebrew Bible the image of the cup of God's wrath is used to indicate the judgement of God on wickedness and idolatry. In Isaiah 51, this image is used to speak of the suffering of God's own people, which, although given by him (verse 17), he himself has taken away (verse 22).

In the Hebrew Bible, the 'cup of wrath' contains the wine that makes people drunk, stagger and fall, never to rise again. In this last verse of 'Child of the stable's secret birth', the content is not the wine of God's wrath but 'all our sorrows, our sins and tears' – echoing the suffering referred to in Isaiah 51. These things also, for a whole variety of reasons, might cause us to fall, never to rise again or, at least, never to hold our heads high.

The second image through which we can unwrap the gift at the heart of today's celebration is that of the 'wayward earth'. The image of a child going off and doing its own thing, conjured up by 'wayward', evokes Jesus' parable of the prodigal son (Luke 15). In his work on Luke's parables, Kenneth Bailey illuminates the cultural background to Jesus' storytelling, which we easily overlook in a Western context. He points out that here neither son has a good relationship with his father. In asking for his share of the inheritance which would not be his until his father's death, the younger son effectively expresses the wish that his father were dead; in accepting his portion, the older son concurs. The older son makes no attempt to bring about reconciliation between his father and brother, as would have been expected. By his actions the younger son breaks the relationship not only with his father but with his whole village community.

However, it is the father's behaviour which is of particular significance today. Twice, he goes out to his sons when he would reasonably have been expected to stay within his house, and does so at great cost to himself – not financial cost but the cost of personal dignity and status. For a Middle Eastern patriarch to run would be to invite derision and a loss of respect in the eyes of the community. Yet when Jesus speaks of the return of the wayward younger son, he describes the action of the father in these terms: 'But while he was still far off, his father saw him and was filled with compassion; he ran and put his arms around him and kissed him' (verse 20). By this action the father demonstrates acceptance and reconciliation, restoring his younger son to his place within the whole community.

Our use of the familiar title, 'the prodigal son', tends to focus attention on the younger son, but the older one is no less of a self-chosen outcast from his father's love. On returning from the fields to the sound of celebration, he does not go and join in but remains outside. Again, the father comes out to him, entreating him to join the party. The father's words emphasize the father–son relationship, yet the older boy speaks as if he sees himself not as a son but as a slave. In this case, his sense of reality is distorted and the father's love refused.

At the start of Advent, we thought about how Christmas can be idealized, with the focus mainly on the sharing – and purchasing – of gifts. We thought about the goodness of this, but also about how it only partially reflects what we are celebrating. Central to this carol of the stable is the conviction that the gift is in Jesus' life, death and resurrection. The burden of those things in the cup, 'all our sorrows, our sins and tears', is taken from us, and we can stand freely. The gift of the Father is evident in the story Jesus tells. When it begins, neither son seems to want a relationship with the father, yet one of them is overwhelmed by the father's humility and excessively generous act of love. The 'prize' that this younger son enjoys is acceptance and inclusion, represented by the father's best robe, the ring, the sandals and the party.

Our prize is cause for a party too: nothing less than the reality of a life where the bounds are bigger than frailty and death; a life to be enjoyed now, and with a fullness yet to come. The gift of the stable is that in opening our lives to the life of the baby, we too are 'ris'n with Christ; at peace with God'.

Postscript: Boxing Day

There has always seemed to me to be a 'cold light of dawn' feel about Boxing Day. As an adult, it is usually a day that brings me a sense of relief. There is no need to get up at a particular time, no one has to do anything, and we can eat leftovers from the day before. As a child, however, I would wake up with a sense of regret. 'It' was over for another whole year, and a year was an unimaginably long time. The build-up of excitement, the anticipation of unwrapping presents, the moment of discovery and tearing of wrappings – it was gone. Everything was out in the open. There was a positive side to all of this though. It was still the school holidays and there was time to enjoy the new things which I had received.

There were still family visits to be enjoyed as well. Boxing Day was my grandmother's birthday, only we were not allowed to call it by its familiar name. The twenty-sixth of December is St Stephen's Day. It was a day when we could sing 'Good King Wenceslas' with a sense of propriety because it tells of something that happened 'on the feast of Stephen'. I was dimly aware that St Stephen had nothing to do with Christmas. In fact, lurking somewhere at the back of my mind was the question of what he was doing there at all. Wasn't Stephen stoned, killed because he stood up for his faith in Jesus? I think I felt rather cross; after all, this was hardly the sort of thing we wanted to be thinking about at Christmas. It spoiled the fun, so I tried not to dwell on it. The trouble was, it was Nanny's birthday, so every year without fail St Stephen had his place.

The childhood me might at one time have sighed over the passing of Christmas, and counted up how many days it would be to the next important celebration. This of course was Easter, with its essential component: chocolate eggs. Nowadays I hope that my perspective is a little different. Easter without chocolate would be bearable; Easter without Jesus would be like many of the eggs – completely hollow.

In the poem I quoted in the Preface, Crashaw refers to the Presentation of Christ in the Temple. This occasion is recounted in Luke's Gospel (Luke 2.22–38), and is celebrated in the church calendar on 2 February. It is part of Luke's nativity story. Luke tells of how Mary and Joseph bring the baby Jesus to the Temple in order to complete the rites of purification set out in the Jewish law (Leviticus 12.1–8). The offering of a lamb or pair of turtle-doves represented cleansing and acceptance before God. This moment in the nativity story marks a turning point in the movement from Christmas to Easter. The elderly Simeon concludes his blessing by warning Mary that 'a sword will pierce your own soul too' (verse 35). If we had not been willing to see it before, then these words make it crystal clear that Jesus' story will be one of suffering.

As I am sure will be clear by now, I think that this aspect of costly suffering is easily buried in the way in which Christmas is anticipated every December. I hope that this book has offered an opportunity to look at the season of Advent afresh. The texts chosen for reflection here help us to see that the direction we are pointed in is towards the Passion, the inevitable outcome of the baby's birth. Crashaw envisages each of us being involved in this journey of sacrifice:

> To Thee, meeke majestie, soft King
> Of simple graces and sweet loves,
> Each of us his Lamb will bring,
> Each his paire of silver doves!
> Till burnt at last, in fire of Thy faire eyes,
> Ourselves become our owne best sacrifice.

In that direction, however, lies resurrection. The traditional 'four last things' of Advent are not about individual destiny so much as about the firm hope of fullness of life, rooted in the resurrection of Jesus, generously offered in the welcoming arms of the Father.

Copyright acknowledgements

Bibliography

Kenneth E. Bailey, *Poet and Peasant and Through Peasant Eyes: A Literary-Cultural Approach to the Parables in Luke* (Combined Edition) (Grand Rapids: Eerdmans, 1983)

Julian Barnes, *A History of the World in 10½ Chapters* (London: Pan-Picador, 1990)

Joseph Blenkinsopp, *Isaiah 55—66: A New Translation with Introduction and Commentary* (The Anchor Yale Bible) (New York: Random House-Doubleday, 2003; New Haven, Conn.: Yale University Press, 2011)

Raymond Brown, *The Gospel According to John I—XII: A New Translation with Introduction and Commentary* (The Anchor Bible) (New York: Random House-Doubleday, 1966, New Haven, Conn.: Yale University Press, 2008)

Raymond Brown, *The Gospel According to John XIII—XXI: A New Translation with Introduction and Commentary* (The Anchor Yale Bible) (New York: Random House-Doubleday 1970)

G. B. Caird, *The Revelation of St John the Divine* (Black's New Testament Commentaries) (London: A & C Black, 1966)

Common Worship: Services and Prayers for the Church of England (London: Church House Publishing, 2000)

Richard Crashaw, 'A Hymne of the Nativity, sung as by the Shepheards', *The Metaphysical Poets* ed. Helen Gardner (Harmondsworth: Penguin, 1957)

Charles Dickens, *A Christmas Carol* (London: Chapman and Hall, 1843)

John Donne, 'Devotions upon Emergent Occasions, Meditation XVII', in *John Donne* (The Oxford Authors) ed. John Carey (Oxford: Oxford University Press, 1990)

Timothy Dudley-Smith, 'Child of the Stable's Secret Birth', *The Oxford Book of Christmas Carols* ed. A. Bullard (Oxford: Oxford University Press, 2009)

Joel B. Green, *The Gospel of Luke* (New International Commentary on the New Testament) (Grand Rapids: Eerdmans, 1997)

Robert H. Gundry, *Matthew: A Commentary on his Handbook for a Mixed Church under Persecution* (Grand Rapids: Eerdmans, 1982)

Tony Harrison, *The Mysteries* (London: Faber & Faber, 1985)

Gerard Manley Hopkins, 'God's Grandeur', in *Gerard Manley Hopkins* (The Oxford Authors) ed. Catherine Phillips (Oxford: Oxford University Press, 1986)

David Lyle Jeffrey (ed.), *A Dictionary of Biblical Tradition in English Literature* (Grand Rapids: Eerdmans, 1992)

C. S. Lewis, *The Voyage of the Dawn Treader* (London: Geoffrey Bles, 1952)

Charles Oakley, 'Hills of the north, rejoice!' (adapted) *Complete Anglican Hymns Old and New* eds Geoffrey Moore, Susan Sayers, Michael Forster and Kevin Mayhew (Buxhall, Stowmarket: Kevin Mayhew, 2000)

John Polkinghorne, *Science and Religion in Quest of Truth* (London: SPCK, 2011)

Earl J. Richard, *First and Second Thessalonians* (Sacra Pagina) (Collegeville, Minn.: Liturgical Press-Michael Glazier, 1995)

Robert Southwell SJ, *Collected Poems* eds Peter Davidson and Anne R. Sweeney (Manchester: FyfieldBooks-Carcanet Press, 2007)

R. S. Thomas, *Counterpoint* (Newcastle upon Tyne: Bloodaxe Books, 1990)

Salley Vickers, *Miss Garnet's Angel* (London: HarperCollins, 2000)

N. T. Wright, *Surprised by Hope: Rethinking Heaven, the Resurrection, and the Mission of the Church* (London: SPCK, 2007)

John Ziesler, *Paul's Letter to the Romans* (PTI New Testament Commentaries) (London: SCM Press, 1989)